Another Look At
The Word And The Sacraments

I0134053

Saving
Grace

Ron Lavin

CSS Publishing Company, Inc., Lima, Ohio

SAVING GRACE

Library of Congress Cataloging-in-Publication Data

Lavin, Ronald J.
    Saving grace : another look at the Word and the sacraments / Ron Lavin.
p. cm.
        ISBN 0-7880-2311-X (pbk. : alk. paper)
    1. Word of God (Theology) 2. Lord's Supper. 3. Baptism. I. Title.
BT180.W67L38 2004
234—dc22

                                                                                2003024647

For more information about CSS Publishing Company resources, visit our website at
www.csspub.com or e-mail us at custserv@csspub.com or call (800) 241-4056.

ISBN 0-7880-2311-X   PRINTED IN U.S.A.

*This book is dedicated to those who worked
with me in Evangelical Outreach*

> *Dick Barclay
> Bob Hock
> Paul Werger
> Amanda Grimmer
> Jim Stephenson
> Dennis Anderson
> Jerry Schmalenberger*
> Pat Smith
> Bill Waxenberg
> Robert Wallace
> and Carl Johnson*

*and to all those dedicated partners and friends
who worked with me on Field Seminaries for
training in evangelism and witness ministries:*

> *Vergil Anderson
> Pat Kiefert
> George Forell
> Lyle Schaller
> Tim Lull
> Larry Smoose
> Sue Torgerson
> and Bill Lazarus.*

*(*Jerry Schmalenberger also worked with me on several of the
Field Seminaries,)*

Books By Ron Lavin

The *Another Look* Series

I Believe; Help My Unbelief: Another Look At The Apostles' Creed
Stories To Remember: Another Look At The Parables Of Jesus
Abba: Another Look At The Lord's Prayer
Saving Grace: Another Look At The Word And The Sacraments

To be published soon:
The Big Ten: Another Look At The Ten Commandments

Other Books In Print

Turning Griping Into Gratitude
Empty Spaces; Empty Places (written with Constance Sorenson)
Way To Grow! (Dynamic Church Growth Through Small Groups)
The Advocate
The Great I AM
Previews Of Coming Attractions

Previously Published Books

Alone / Together
You Can't Start A Car With A Cross
You Can Grow In A Small Group
Jesus In Stained Glass
Jesus Christ, The Liberator (written with Bill Grimmer, M.D.)
Hey, Mom, Look At Me!

JUSTICE means getting what you deserve.

MERCY means not getting what you deserve.

GRACE means getting what you do not deserve.

Some of the Pharisees in the crowd said to Jesus, "Teacher, rebuke your disciples!"

"I tell you," he replied, "if they keep quiet, the stones will cry out."

— Luke 19:39-40

Table Of Contents

A Personal Word
About The *Another Look* Series

Saving Grace is the fourth book in the *Another Look* series. The first book in this series was *I Believe; Help My Unbelief: Another Look At The Apostles' Creed*; the second was *Stories To Remember: Another Look At The Parables Of Jesus*; the third was *Abba: Another Look At The Lord's Prayer*. The fifth book in this series is *The Big Ten: Another Look At The Ten Commandments*. *Saving Grace* is about the word of God and the sacraments.

The saving grace of God in word and sacraments was the theme of Evangelical Outreach (EO) in the 1970s and 1980s. I was privileged to be the Pastor Director of EO and then a consultant and pastor-evangelist for the movement. Paul Werger, Bob Hock, Jim Stephenson, Dick Barclay, Amanda Grimmer, Bill Waxenberg, Dennis Anderson, Pat Smith, and many other pastor-evangelists and I spoke at Synod conventions, pastors' conferences, evangelism events, and churches of all shapes and sizes. We spoke of Gospel-centered outreach to those who were outsiders to the Christian faith. We spoke of the power of word and sacraments to change and sustain our lives.

In the 1990s the topics of word and sacraments were a central part of the thirteen Field Seminaries that were conducted across the country by a group of theologians, seminary presidents, pastors, and lay leaders of which I was privileged to be a part. Some of the other leaders were Pat Kiefert, Bill Lazarus, George Forell, Jerry Schmalenberger, Tim Lull, Lyle Schaller, Larry Smoose, Sue Torgerson, and Vergil Anderson. Many of the insights I gained into the basics of the Christian faith came from these wise and dedicated friends.

The American Field Seminaries were patterned after the one in Tanzania, Africa, which I had an opportunity to observe in person in 1975. The African model teaches the basics of our faith with a special focus on application to real life situations. The American model has the same goal.

In other words, in the Field Seminary we focus on practical theology. That is the spirit in which all of the books in the *Another Look* series were written. That is particularly true for *Saving Grace*. There are two questions we should ask about every book, including this one: 1) Is it true? and 2) What difference does it make? I pray what is said here about word and sacraments is true. In addition, I hope that the book makes a difference in the way in which the Gospel of Jesus Christ is shared, proclaimed, and received.

In the twenty-first century there is a need for a major emphasis on God's word, Baptism into the kingdom, and the kingdom Eucharist. In seeking relevance some churches have put these basics on the margin of church life. Isn't it time to get back to the basics of our faith? What could be more basic than the word of God and the sacraments, God's holy pipelines from heaven?

In his book *The Proclamation Of The Gospel In A Pluralistic World*, George Forell calls us to proclamation of the one true Gospel. He also urges us to take seriously that the pluralistic world in which we live has a challenging set of variables, ideas, ideologies, and beliefs. In other words, we must both proclaim the truth (the text) and learn the context of people's lives today. What is the context into which Christian truth about word and sacraments is declared and shared?

In writing *Saving Grace*, I expressed some of the basic teachings of our faith in the context of the life of Grace Livingstone, a composite fictional character. It is my hope that the vignettes about Grace will assist the reader to see the complicated, pluralistic context of the lives of many people today. Grace is like many outsiders I have met in the course of 44 years of ministry. She is an outsider who doesn't even know enough about the Christian faith to make an intelligent rejection of it. In addition, since she doesn't accept herself, she is an outsider who feels there is no way she could be accepted in a Christian community. Can this outsider and thousands like her be drawn into the word and sacrament community called the Church? That is not only the challenge of writing this book, but the challenge all Christians have before them to witness to outsiders today.

I believe the Church exists not only to sustain those who believe, but to reach out to those who do not belong. The preaching of the word and celebration of the sacraments appear to outsiders to be meaningless rituals, totally out of touch with the real world of making a living, paying bills, keeping a marriage or other relationship from falling apart, staying healthy, or raising kids in a time when traditional values are marginalized at best, and at worst dismissed altogether.

Can *Saving Grace* and the other books in the *Another Look* series contribute to the movement of evangelical outreach today? Can these books make a significant difference in people's lives? Can these books reach out and touch someone with the Gospel? Can the books in the *Another Look* series help people overcome illusions about what Christians believe? I hope so. Maybe these books can even help so-called atheists.

If someone tells you, "I don't believe in God," you might consider this response. "Tell me about the god you don't believe in. Chances are, I don't believe in that god either." The god people "don't believe in" is generally miles apart from the God and Father of our Lord Jesus Christ. The god people "don't believe in" is often an illusion.

Can people be better informed about what Christians really believe and how to apply the time-tested truths of faith to our lives today? I believe so. That is why I have written the *Another Look* series. I certainly do not have all the answers to the questions people are asking today, but I hope the books in this series will be helpful in some ways to some people. Do people hunger for the word and sacraments? Yes, I believe they do. That is why I wrote *Saving Grace*.

Ron Lavin
Encinitas, California
randjlavin@cox.net

Introduction

The kingdom of God is the theme of the books in the *Another Look* series. Here in *Saving Grace* we focus on the word and sacraments as pipelines from the kingdom of God to earth. Of course, the kingdom of God does not come in fullness until the end of time when every knee will bow before the Lord Jesus Christ, but in this life we can get previews of coming attractions.

The word of God, Baptism, and the Lord's Supper give us a foretaste of the fullness of the kingdom. Specifically, when we are baptized, the kingdom comes. When the word of God reaches our hearts by grace through faith, we turn from other priorities to God as our highest priority. That's the kingdom of God at work. The kingdom comes to us as a foretaste as we receive bread and wine in Holy Communion. God's saving grace is at work in word and sacraments. *Saving Grace* is all about these breakthroughs.

This book is intended for personal inspiration, growth, and understanding, but it is also intended for group use. Questions and the Digging Deeper section at the end of each chapter will assist a wide variety of groups in their study, fellowship, and application of the word to life. Before teaching or leading a group on this material, group leaders and teachers should look at the section in the back of the book titled Tips For Pastors, Group Leaders, And Teachers. This section should help a group leader or teacher with preparation for using this book.

Bible study groups, new members' classes, adult Sunday School classes, or small groups meeting in church or homes will help Christians apply biblical truths to their lives. We need encouragement. We need support. There is no panacea for what is wrong with the church today, but I believe that small groups of Christians meeting to study and apply God's word to their lives can make a major step forward. Through small groups, the saving grace of God may reach out and touch the lives of many people who think of the church, if at all, only in institutional terms.

In the twenty-first century two movements are at the forefront for Christians: small groups and lay ministry development. Small church groups go by many names including koinonia (fellowship) groups, growth groups, prayer groups, and yokefellow groups. One common denominator of these groups is lay ministry development.

Twenty-first century Christians, like those in the first century, can find their spiritual gifts, use their gifts, and step forward in the leadership of God's church. My emphasis on lay leadership in no way diminishes the importance of clergy. As lay people step forward and become partners with pastors, the saving grace of God goes out with power to unbelievers and outsiders.

Outsiders are shocked when people's lives are actually changed by God. They sit up and take notice of the power of the gospel when ordinary people become extraordinary through the power of the word and sacraments. The word and sacraments make ordinary people extraordinary. The word and sacraments make a real difference in people's lives.

You, the reader, can expect a Lutheran perspective on word and sacraments in this book. After all, I am a Lutheran pastor. But there is a growing consensus among all Christians, from Roman Catholics to Reformed Protestants, about the power of both of these channels of God's grace. That consensus is reflected in *Saving Grace*.

A special "thank you" is offered my many partners and the participants in Evangelical Outreach, the movement within the Lutheran Church In America, of which I was Director-Director for a number of years. In addition, "thanks" go to the teaching partners in the thirteen Field Seminaries we conducted throughout the United States. These partners and Field Seminary participants taught me volumes about the holiness of the word and sacraments and how practical application can emerge from focusing on what God has given us in his pipelines from heaven.

Barbara Coulson, President of the Southern California Writers' Association, proof-read the manuscript of *Saving Grace*. Her many suggested changes sent me back to the task of revision and clarification. Thanks, Barbara, you made a positive contribution to this book.

George Forell is not only a special mentor and friend, but in my lifetime has been one of the leading theologians in the United

States. Thanks, George, for your insights and dedication to telling the truth as you see it forthrightly and clearly.

The Bible translation used in *Saving Grace* is generally the *New International Version* (NIV). Where other translations are used, the source is noted.

Prologue

Grace Livingstone was not a good driver. Her father told her, "You're thirty years old. By now you should know how to drive." Her live-in boyfriend said it more harshly, "You're a menace on the road."

Grace looked into the rearview mirror too often. She lacked focus on what was ahead because she was always looking back. She had gotten into three auto accidents in the past year because of being fearful and distracted by what was behind her and around her.

One day as she was driving past a big church in her home town of Davenport, Iowa, she glanced sideways. Then she studied the church in the rear view mirror. *I really should get back to church one of these days*, she thought. She quickly looked forward and realized she had almost failed to see a pedestrian who was crossing in a crosswalk. She jammed on the brakes and stopped inches from the old woman who jumped sideways to avoid being hit. *That was a close call*, she thought. "Sorry," she yelled out the window. "Really sorry. I hope you aren't hurt." She had not hit the woman, yet the woman had fallen and was on the ground, holding her hip.

Sarah Williams was coming from church where she had been praying. She had a lot on her mind. Her grandson was in trouble with the law again. He was an alcoholic and when he drank, he got mean. He had gotten into a fight with a smaller man at a bar and had broken his jaw. "I'm okay," she shouted.

Grace pulled her car over to the side of the street and stopped. "I don't know what distracted me," she said. "I should have been watching more closely. I hope you aren't hurt."

17

"Just my pride, dear."

"Can I drive you to a hospital?"

"No need. My hip hurts a little from the fall, but it will be okay. I'm tough."

"At least let me drive you home."

"I can just catch a bus. The bus line runs right by my house."

"No need for you to take a bus. I'm not going anywhere. I can give you a lift."

Grace and Sarah made small talk in the car on the way to Sarah's house. "I'm so sorry," Grace said. If she said it once, she said it fifteen times.

An inordinate number of apologies usually indicates inferiority, Sarah thought. *I should really try to help this woman.* "Can you come in for a spot of tea?" Sarah asked when they arrived in front of the old, but neat brick house.

"If it isn't too much trouble, I'd love a cup of tea. I don't have anywhere special I have to go."

After tea and cookies were served, Sarah asked, "Do you have a church, dear?"

"No. No, I don't. As a matter of fact, I was distracted by looking sideways and then backwards at that big church where you were walking."

"That's my church," Sarah said with a smile. "Lots of good folks there. Would you like to come to a women's Bible study with me at our church sometime?"

Section One:

The Word Of God

Chapter One

Plans For Your Welfare

*"... Surely I know the plans I have for you, says the
LORD, plans for your welfare and not for harm, to
give you a future with hope."*　　　— Jeremiah 29:11

Listen to me, you islands;
*　　hear this, you distant nations:*
Before I was born the LORD called me;
*　　from my birth he has made mention of my name.*
He made my mouth like a sharpened sword,
*　　in the shadow of his hand he hid me;*
he made me into a polished arrow
*　　and concealed me in his quiver.*
He said to me, "You are my servant,
*　　Israel, in whom I will display my splendor."*
But I said, "I have labored to no purpose;
*　　I have spent my strength in vain and for nothing.*
Yet what is due me is in the LORD's hand,
*　　and my reward is with my God."*

And now the LORD says —
*　　he who formed me in the womb to be his servant*
to bring Jacob back to him
*　　and gather Israel to himself,*
for I am honored in the eyes of the LORD
*　　and my God has been my strength —*
he says:

21

*"It is too small a thing for you to be my servant
to restore the tribes of Jacob
and bring back those of Israel I have kept.
I will also make you a light for the Gentiles,
that you may bring my salvation to the ends of the earth."*
— Isaiah 49:1-6

These two texts provide an excellent example of how the word[1] of God takes three forms in our lives. The first form is Jesus himself. In the first chapter of the Gospel of John we read, "The Word[2] became flesh and made his dwelling among us" (John 1:14). In the Jeremiah and the Isaiah texts we have prophecy about Israel being restored, but these passages also point beyond their historical setting to the future Redeemer, Jesus Christ. The Gospel of John says, "In him was life, and that life was the light of men" (John 1:4). Jesus said, "I am the light of the world" (John 8:12).

Jesus is the Word through whom all things were made. This pre-existent Word became flesh and blood, son of Mary. At age thirty he left home and started his ministry as the light shining brightly and overcoming the darkness for all kinds of people — Jews and Gentiles alike.

Saint Paul, the Apostle, writes:

He is the image of the invisible God, the firstborn over all creation. For by him all things were created: things in heaven and on earth, visible and invisible, whether thrones or powers or rulers or authorities; all things were created by him and for him. He is before all things, and in him all things hold together.
— Colossians 1:15-17

In other words, Jesus, the Word of God, enlightens the entire world (people of all colors and kinds) with his light. He is the instrument of creation, and all things find their fulfillment in him. He is the glue that holds all things together. As the Word made flesh, he invites people into a new way of life. "From the fullness of his grace we have all received one blessing after another" (John 1:16). Saving grace is at work in the person of Jesus. First and foremost, Jesus is the Word of God.

The second form of the word of God is Scriptures. For the early Christians what we call the Old Testament was that word. Later, the letters of Paul and others and the four Gospels came to be regarded as Scriptures as well.

When believers read Scriptures, individually or in groups, the word can become alive for them. In other words, Bible passages can lead people to the saving grace of God through faith in Jesus Christ.

If people come to believe that God has plans for their welfare, not their harm, and that they are given a future with hope by the grace of God, they will want others to know about this salvation. They will bring salvation "to the ends of the earth." In the early church, bringing this salvation through Christ to all people everywhere was called preaching. Preaching was not limited to an ordained preacher in a pulpit of a church building on Sunday mornings. All Christians saw themselves as God's witnesses.

The third form the word of God takes is preaching in this larger sense. *Declaring* and *sharing* the story of Jesus changes people's lives. Not all of God's people are flaming evangelists. Some are witnesses in everyday life in quieter ways. Some d*eclare*; others *share* more quietly as opportunity presents itself. Jeremiah and Isaiah were *declarers,* called to be lights for the world. Jesus and his apostles were *declarers,* called to be lights shining in the world. "Don't hide your light under a bushel basket," Jesus said. He obviously expected all of his followers to do something about the light he had given them. Called Pastors are given the commission to bring light to darkness. When they preach, they are called to *declare* the good news of salvation through Jesus Christ. In addition, all Christians are called to bring light to the darkness by *sharing* the Word of God with people as opportunity presents itself.

Grace Livingstone was listening to the pastor of Messiah Lutheran Church talk about these two Old Testament passages. She was at a women's Bible study with her new friend Sarah Williams. After the pastor offered a prayer, Sarah asked Grace how she had done during the study.

"I'm ashamed to say it, but I didn't get what he was saying at all. I don't even know what the Old Testament is. He seems like a nice enough fellow, but he really snowed me with terms like 'Gentile,' 'grace,' 'salvation,' and 'the Word made flesh.' I really feel out of place here. All of you know so much. I don't know anything. If the pastor had called on me, I would have died. I would have run out of the room crying. This Bible study was a real challenge for me. I'm so dumb about religious things."

Just then, one of the women in the Bible study came over to where Grace and Sarah were sitting in the back of the room. "I'd like to introduce myself. I'm Mary Anderson." Looking at Grace's name tag, Mary added, "I see your name is Grace. What a lovely name. Welcome. Can you stay for coffee or tea? I'd like to introduce you to our pastor."

"I'm sorry," Grace said barely above a whisper, "but I have to run along. Thanks for inviting me." Grace rushed out the door.

I don't want to meet the pastor, she thought. *I'm feeling all closed in. What am I getting myself in for? I thought I might want to come back to church. Now I don't think so. My life is empty and I need something. I thought it might be God. Maybe not, if I have to learn about Jeremiah and Isaiah. I feel embarrassed. Ashamed. Ignorant. Sarah and her friend Mary are nice. Why should I feel this way?*

Mary said to Sarah, "I like your new friend, but I think she's feeling overwhelmed and fearful. When I first came to church, I felt that way, too. Is there anything we can do to help her?"

"I'll phone her later and see if I can help," Sarah replied. "All of us have fears we have to overcome. Maybe she will share some of hers with me."

Questions For Personal Consideration
And/Or Group Discussion

1. After reading about Grace and Sarah in the prologue and chapter one, how would you describe the kinds of people they are?

    Grace   Sarah

    _____   _____

    _____   _____

    _____   _____

2. If you were Sarah, what would you say to Grace after her negative experience at that Bible study?

3. If you were the pastor, how could you have presented the material in a more "user friendly" way for a person like Grace?

4. If you were Grace, how would you feel about Mary's greeting and invitation?

Digging Deeper

1. Since both Jeremiah 19:11 and Isaiah 49:1-6 were written for the Jews years ago, what are the pros and cons regarding applying them to Christians today?

2. Name some kinds of people today who are outsiders like the Gentiles in the Bible.

3. Isaiah 49:6 says that it is a small thing to be a servant and a greater thing to be a light to the Gentiles. In what ways is it a greater thing to be a light to the Gentiles?

4. Is anyone today called "before they were born" (Isaiah 49:1)?

5. What is the difference between a *declarer* and a *sharer*?

Chapter Two

Your Word Is A Lamp To My Feet

Oh, how I love your law!
I meditate on it all day long.
Your commands make me wiser than my enemies,
for they are ever with me.
I have more insight than all my teachers,
for I meditate on your statutes.
I have kept my feet from every evil path
so that I might obey your word.
I have not departed from your laws,
for you yourself have taught me.
How sweet are your words to my taste,
sweeter than honey to my mouth!
I gain understanding from your precepts;
therefore I hate every wrong path.

Your word is a lamp to my feet
and a light for my path.

I have taken an oath and confirmed it
that I will follow your righteous laws.
I have suffered much;
preserve my life, O LORD, according to your word.
Accept, O LORD, the willing praise of my mouth,
and teach me your laws.
Though I constantly take my life in my hands,
I will not forget your law.
— Psalm 119:97-109

Psalm 119 is the longest Psalm in the Bible. It has 176 verses. Most of these verses are about the laws of God. The theme is the psalmist's love of the law of God. At first glance, we might dismiss this Psalm as having too much law!

But hints of what we have come to call the gospel are sprinkled throughout the 176 verses. Consider the following examples.

Verse 10: "I will seek you with all my heart...." The psalmist's vision of God is largely of a God of law, yet matters of his heart reach out beyond this limited vision.

Verse 25: "I am laid low in the dust; preserve my life according to your word." Mercy, not just law, is needed when we are laid low.

Verse 28: "My soul is weary with sorrow; strengthen me according to your word" and verse 156: "Your compassion is great, O LORD...." These verses sound like pleas to the compassionate God.

Verse 41: "May your unfailing love come to me, O LORD, your salvation according to your promise ..." and verse 124: "Deal with your servant according to your love...." Unfailing love, salvation, and promise are words that are usually associated with the gospel, not the law.

Verse 49: "Remember your word to your servant, for you have given me hope." Hope comes from the God of love.

Verse 76: "May your unfailing love be my comfort, according to your promise to your servant. Let your compassion come to me that I may live...." The gospel clearly makes us dependent on God's unfailing love, comfort, and compassion.

Verse 89: "Your word, O LORD, is eternal; it stands firm in the heavens." Doesn't that eternal word of God include fatherly encouragement and approval as well as laws?

Verse 94: "Save me, for I am yours...." Sounds like a plea for the gospel of grace to me.

The text before us, Psalm 119:94-107, is mostly about the psalmist's love for the law of God, but in this Psalm we also find hints of the gospel of the Lord Jesus Christ. For example, verse 103 says, "How sweet are your words to my taste, sweeter than honey to my mouth!" The crowning jewel of Psalm 119 is verse 105: *"Your word is a lamp to my feet and a light to my path."*

As Christians, we know the words of Jesus about forgiveness and grace are sweet to hear and taste. In sermons and Bible studies, we hear this word that lights up our lives and our pathways. In Holy Communion we taste forgiveness and grace. As Christians, we know that by his life, death on the cross, and his resurrection, Jesus has shown us the light for the journey we make in life.

The psalmist brings us to our knees with guilt about having broken the laws of God, but there are enough hints of the gospel here to raise us up again to stand at full stature before the God of mercy and grace.

Grace Livingstone was sitting next to Sarah in the back of the church. She had come because Sarah had invited her, but she was confused. The psalmist loved the law of God (v. 97). She hated it. The psalmist had kept his feet from every evil path (v. 101). She had walked in the paths of evil since she was a teenager — drinking, taking drugs, having illicit sex, and lying time and again. She was feeling very uncomfortable, guilt-ridden but with no place to go and no will left to change.

The psalmist had taken an oath before God and confirmed it (v. 106). Grace had attended a church as a child, but had lost contact with God and church long ago. The psalmist had *not* forgotten God's law (v. 109). She remembered some of the Ten Commandments, but forgot them when temptations came. He was hopeful; she hopeless. He was faithful. This was her first time in church for years. *And my last time*, she thought.

The preacher's references to hints of the gospel in Psalm 119 did not touch her at all. She had to get away from all this religious talk. She couldn't take it anymore. Just as she was about to get up and leave, the preacher said, "Let me tell you a story about how the gospel works."

She liked stories. Maybe this one would make her feel better.

The pastor told the congregation that the story was told by a speaker he had recently heard at a conference. "Brennan Manning is a renegade Catholic priest who got married," Pastor Jeff said. "He is one of the most dynamic speakers for God I have heard. He speaks to Catholics, Protestants, and people on the edges of faith. Manning's story is about a man who almost gave up on religion because he didn't know how to pray. It is also a story about the gospel."[3]

An old man was dying of cancer. His daughter asked her priest to come to visit him. When the priest arrived, he noticed an empty chair by the man's bedside and commented to the man that he must have realized that he was coming and provided a place for him to sit.

"Please close the door," the dying man said to the priest.

Puzzled, the priest shut the door.

"I've never told anyone this, not even my daughter," said the old man, "but all of my life I have never known how to pray. At Sunday Mass I used to hear the pastor talk about prayer, but his words went over my head. Finally, one day I told him that I got nothing out of his sermons on prayer. He reached into a desk drawer and gave me a book on prayer. I tried to read it, but I had to look up twelve words in the first three pages. I gave the book back to him.

"I abandoned any attempt at prayer," he continued, "until one day my best friend told me, 'Joe, prayer is just a simple matter of having a conversation with Jesus. Here's what I suggest. Sit down on a chair, place an empty chair in front of you, and in faith see Jesus on that chair. It's not spooky, because he promised to be with us. Just talk to him and listen the same way you're doing with me right now.'

"So, Padre, I tried it and I liked it. I do it a couple of hours every day. I'm careful though. If my daughter saw me talking to an empty chair, she'd either have a nervous breakdown or send me off to the funny farm."

The priest was impressed with the story and encouraged the old man to continue his journey in prayer. They prayed together, and the priest left.

Two nights later the daughter called and told the priest that her daddy had died that afternoon. "Did he die in peace?" the priest asked.

"Yes, when I left the house around two o'clock, he called me over to his bedside, told me one of his corny jokes, and kissed me on the cheek. When I got back from the store an hour later, I found him dead. But there was something strange, Father. In fact beyond strange, kind of weird. Apparently just before Daddy died, he leaned over and rested his head on a chair beside his bed."

As the pastor finished the story, Grace was crying again. These were different tears than the ones shed when she heard about the law. Sarah Williams was sitting next to her. She reached over and touched her hand. Then she took out a tissue and gave it to Grace.

Grace wiped her eyes and her nose and said in a broken voice, "That was a wonderful story. I know what it is like not to be able to pray. I can't really change, but thanks for trying."

Sarah reached over and put her arm around Grace. "God loves you," she said. "Give it time. There's no rush. God can change you. When you pray, just think about talking to an old friend."

"I don't have any friends," Grace muttered.

I don't have time for friends. Friends are too demanding. Friends interfere with your life. When I was a little girl, I had friends. What happened?

Then the congregation sang the hymn, "What A Friend We Have In Jesus." From across the aisle, Mary Anderson caught Grace's eye and smiled.

When Grace got home, her live-in boyfriend didn't smile.

"Where you been?" Jake demanded.

"Church."

"Church?" he said with a snicker. "You dummy. All they want is your money. There's no God. Church is for weaklings and losers who can't make it on their own."

"You're the dummy. You're the loser. You don't even have a job."

"Not my fault! They fired me for no reason at all."

"They fired you because of your drinking."

"Enough. Don't bring that up again. It's none of your damn business."

"It's my business since you live here in my house."

31

"I'm going for a walk. Maybe I'll never come back."

"Good."

When Jake returned, he threw in his hat first. Then he gave Grace a present, a cheap rhinestone ring. He also bought himself a present. A quart of whiskey.

Questions For Personal Consideration And/Or Group Discussion

1. Do you agree or disagree with the statement, "The laws of the Bible are all good commands we should never break."

2. Why do outsiders feel so strange when they first come to church?

3. In sermons and Bible studies we sometimes hear words that light up our lives. Can you name some times when this was true for you?

4. Sometimes friends are God's messengers, saying the right thing at the right time in the right way. Can you recall times when this was true for you?

5. Do you know anyone like Grace Livingstone? Describe that person.

6. Do you know anyone like Sarah Williams? Describe that person.

Digging Deeper

1. Psalm 119 may have been written by Ezra after the Temple was rebuilt (Ezra 6:14-15) as a repetitive meditation on the beauty of God's word. This psalm has 22 carefully constructed sections, each corresponding to a different letter in the Hebrew alphabet. Almost every verse mentions God's word.

2. Most of us chafe under the rules, thinking that they will keep us from doing what we want to do. If we understand that God's laws are for our good, is it possible that this attitude will change?

3. How can the psalmist claim that he loves the laws of God?

4. How can we avoid getting sucked into the impure cultural environment around us?

5. What Bible verses are lamps or lights for your pathway?

6. 1 Peter 1:23 says, "For you have been born again, not of perishable seed but of imperishable, through the living and enduring word of God."

Chapter Three

Saved By The Word

"The word is near you; it is in your mouth and in your heart,"[4] that is, the word of faith we are proclaiming: That if you confess with your mouth, "Jesus is Lord," and believe in your heart that God raised him from the dead, you will be saved. For it is with your heart that you believe and are justified, and it is with your mouth that you confess and are saved. As the Scripture says, "Anyone who trusts in him will never be put to shame."[5] For there is no difference between Jew and Gentile — the same Lord is Lord of all and richly blesses all who call on him, for, "Everyone who calls on the name of the Lord will be saved."[6]

How, then, can they call on the one they have not believed in? And how can they believe in the one of whom they have not heard? And how can they hear without someone preaching to them? And how can they preach unless they are sent? As it is written, "How beautiful are the feet of those who bring good news."[7]

But not all the Israelites accepted the good news. For Isaiah says, "Lord, who has believed our message?"[8] Consequently, faith comes from hearing the message, and the message is heard through the word of Christ.   — Romans 10:8b-17

In this Bible passage we meet Saint Paul's clear vision of salvation through the word of God. The confession "Jesus is Lord" (Romans 10:9) is the first Christian creed. When a person makes that sincere confession in his or her heart, that person has begun the journey of faith. This faith is primarily trust in and dependence on God rather than self. To depend on God for salvation is the one thing needful and the hardest thing of all.

Saint Paul then goes on to explain how people receive this word of God. He asks four questions:

1. How can people call on the name of Christ if they have never known him?
2. How can they believe in Christ if they have never heard about him?
3. How can they hear without someone preaching to them?
4. How can people preach if they are not sent?

First, people must hear about Jesus Christ. We are called to be witnesses for him in our everyday lives. To the apostles, the risen and ascending Christ said, "... You will be my witnesses in Jerusalem, and in all Judea and Samaria, and to the ends of the earth" (Acts 1:8). Think of four concentric circles. Start where you are. Then go out further and further.

All the ends of the earth

Samaria

Judea

Jerusalem

Start in your Jerusalem. The apostles were in Jerusalem when they heard this message about witnessing. For us, Jerusalem means our families and close friends. To witness means to share what you know. Can't we share the gospel of Christ with people with whom we are close?

Next go to Judea. Judea was the surrounding countryside around Jerusalem. For us Judea means people in the neighborhood and at work. Watch for openings, times of need. Be ready to share faith when people need it. A woman down the block is going through a divorce. Invite her to talk about how she feels. Be a good listener. Ask her if she has a church or if she has faith to strengthen her in this hour of need. A man gets a promotion at work. Praise him and ask him to tell you about his new position. God may provide you with just the right opening. Points of change — good or bad — can be openings to share faith.

After Judea, Samaria is mentioned. Samaria was the territory of the people who were different. When the Babylonians conquered Judea in 586 B.C., they deported the strong Jews to Babylon. Those Jews who were left settled in an area called Samaria, inter-married with the Gentiles, lost their focus on monotheism, and compromised their morality. When the Jews returned to Judea, they avoided the territory of the Samaritans like the plague. In contrast, Jesus told a parable called The Good Samaritan. He also converted a Samaritan woman and then the people in her town (John 4:1-42). The way to witness in Samaria is to speak to people who are unlike us in color, economic status, religious background, and other ways.

Jesus told his followers to witness for him to the ends of the earth. He assured them, "And surely I am with you always, to the very end of the age" (Matthew 28:20). What does this mean for us? It means he will be with us as we witness for Christ without geographic limits. Where we can't personally go, we need to be sure that missionaries go to introduce people to Jesus Christ.

The first task is to introduce people to Jesus. The second is to invite them to believe in him as Lord. People everywhere need to hear about the possibility of belief and what it means. As in the case of introducing people to Jesus, helping them to come to faith starts where we are, moves out to the people nearby, then out to people unlike us and finally to the ends of the earth.

Third, the word of God must be preached. All Christians are called to *share* the gospel of Christ as witnesses. Some are called to *declare*, to preach the gospel. Saint Paul puts it this way: "We have different gifts, according to the grace given us. If a man's gift is prophesying (foretelling or forth-telling, usually called preaching), let him use it in proportion to his faith" (Romans 12:6).

In other words, not everyone is called to be a pastor, an evangelist, a missionary or a prophet, but those who are so called are invited to set forth the gospel with the power of the faith God has provided.

In 1 Corinthians 12:4, Saint Paul says the same thing in different words. "There are different kinds of gifts, but the same Spirit. There are different kinds of service, but the same Lord. There are different kinds of working, but the same God works all of them in all men."

Again he lists prophesy as one of the gifts of the Spirit. Some have one gift; some another. Some Christians, not all, are called to be preachers and evangelists, but all are called to be witnesses.

Fourth, if a Christian is a preacher or evangelist, Saint Paul says it must be because of the call. The preacher must be sent. That call comes to people in a wide variety of ways, but one thing is certain: without a call, no one should be a preacher of the word. Pastors who are not in the ministry because of being sent by God are false prophets.

Even when churches have called and sent pastors preaching the word of God with passion and sincerity, not everyone comes to faith. As Saint Paul said, "Not all the Israelites accepted the good news" (Romans 10:16). Some don't understand it. Some refuse to believe it because of their hardness of heart. Some say they believe it, but refuse to change their lives and thus lose whatever small gains they have made in faith. That's the bad news.

On the other hand, the good news is some believe and are saved. We are saved by God's grace, through faith. This is not of ourselves. It is a gift of God — not of works, so that no one can boast (Ephesians 2:8).

Grace Livingstone listened intently as the seminary professor finished his Bible lecture by asking, "Are there any questions?" Mary Anderson, Grace's new friend from the women's Bible study group, had persuaded Grace to come to this lecture at her church. Grace was reluctant, but Mary was persistent. Mary leaned over close to Grace and asked in a whisper, "Grace, do you have any questions?"

"Dozens, but I could never ask them here."

"Why not?"

"I'd just make a fool of myself," Grace replied.

"Let's go for coffee after the questions," Mary said. "We can talk privately there."

"Okay."

A man in the front row asked the lecturer the first question: "What do you believe about conversion? Does it have to take place when you are an adult and can make a decision for Christ, or does it begin in infant Baptism?"

The professor cleared his throat and answered the question in theological terms that were way over Grace's head. He said something about infant Baptism being the born again experience the Bible talks about, but added, "For some people, this doesn't happen until they are adults."

Grace closed her eyes and tried to think, but she just didn't get it. *Conversion? Born again? Baptism? I've got to get out of here. I'm really in way over my head*, she thought.

Several other questions were asked and answered. There was a round of polite applause as the lecturer finished up and the hostess for the event, Grace's new friend Sarah Williams, announced that coffee and home-made cookies were available in the back of Fellowship Hall.

Grace made for the door. Mary was close behind her. When they got outside, Grace took a deep breath of the night air to try to clear her head. "The coffee shop is only a block away," Mary said, hopefully.

"I've only got 45 minutes, but I guess we can go," Grace replied. They walked quickly and without a word to the coffee shop.

"Grace," Mary said when they sat down, "do you feel you can share any of your questions with me? I'd be glad to help in any way I can." Before Grace could answer, the waiter came and asked for their order. They both ordered coffee, black.

"I don't even know enough about the Bible and religion to ask intelligent questions," Grace blurted out. "I appreciate your inviting me to this lecture, but the professor and his theology were Greek to me. I attended a church a few times as a child, but I haven't had any schooling in Christianity."

"Yet you have come to the women's Bible study and to worship once, and you came tonight. That's a good start. You must be looking for something."

"I guess I know something's missing in my life, but I don't know what it is. My father is sick. The doctor says that he may not make it. Lately I've been thinking I should really get some information about God. I feel so ignorant."

"Can you tell me what you didn't understand tonight? Maybe I can clarify it a little."

"Who is this Saint Paul the professor talked so much about?"

Mary explained the story of Saul, the persecutor of Christians, who became Paul, the apostle. "He was converted on the road to Damascus," she said.

"What does 'converted' mean?"

"It means changing directions. Saul was doing what he thought was right by arresting and killing Christians, but the Lord stopped him when he was going to a city called Damascus and turned him around. He was going the wrong way. God stopped him and sent him on the right way, God's way. Paul became the leader of Christianity in the first century. He wrote many letters to churches he started. Many of them are in the Bible."

"Letters?"

"Romans, Ephesians, and the Corinthian letters are examples."

"So that's what the professor was quoting when he used these terms?"

"Right."

"Are people still converted today?"

"Yes, Grace. People who are going the wrong direction away from God can be turned around and head back to God."

"That's hard to believe."

"A lot of people find it hard to believe, but it's true. I know. It happened to me. I know you have to run, but when you have time, I'd like to tell you how God has changed my life."

You're nice, Mary, but I don't want to hear how your life has been changed by God. Good for you, but don't try to change me. I can't change. I'm afraid to change.

40

Questions For Personal Consideration And/Or Group Discussion

1. Why would someone like Grace come to a Bible lecture in a church?

2. What does "the word is near you; it is in your mouth and in your heart" (Romans 10:8b) mean?

3. Can you identify the various places for witnessing in your life based on Acts 1:8?
   a. Jerusalem
   b. Judea
   c. Samaria
   d. The ends of the earth

4. What do you think Mary Anderson did right in witnessing to Grace Livingstone?

5. Do you think Mary did anything wrong in her attempt to witness to Grace?

Digging Deeper

1. This chapter is about salvation. The Bible uses this term not only to mean what happens to believers after they die, but what happens in this life as well. Salvation from our enemies, from sickness, from evil spirits, and from sins are just a few of the ways the Bible speaks of salvation.

2. In the Old Testament, salvation means "to be wide, spacious, or without hindrance and thus to ultimately have victory."[9] Over the years, the word came to mean deliverance from danger and tyranny or rescue from peril.

3. In the New Testament, about one-fifth of the 150 instances where the words "save" or "salvation" are used refer to a salvation to be consummated at the last day (e.g. Romans 13:11; 1 Peter 1:5; 1 Thessalonians 5:8).[10]

4. Matthew 1:21 states that the purpose of Jesus' ministry is to save people from their sins.

5. Nearly a third of the New Testament references to salvation denote deliverance from specific ills such as captivity, disease, and devil possession (e. g. Matthew 9:21 and Luke 8:36).[11]

Chapter Four

Not Ashamed Of The Gospel

*I am not ashamed of the gospel, because it is the power
of God for salvation of everyone who believes; first
for the Jew, then for the Gentile. For in the gospel a
righteousness from God is revealed, a righteousness
that is by faith from first to last, just as it is written:
"The righteous will live by faith."*[12]

— Romans 1:16-17

Grace said, "No, sorry, I can't make it," to Mary Anderson's
invitation to come to her house for coffee. When Mary asked a
third time, Grace felt that she could not put it off again. It just
wasn't polite. *I can always get up and leave*, she thought.

"Glad you could make it," a cheery Mary said at the door. "It's
been a couple of weeks since we last talked. I'm happy you could
come."

After some small talk, Mary said, "How's your life going these
days?"

That question surprised Grace. She expected a lecture. Mary
seemed genuinely interested in her.

"Well, not so good, I guess. My dad is still very ill. The doctor
says that he may not have long to live. It's cancer. I'm so fearful. I
just don't know what will happen."

"You really love him, don't you?"

Grace took a swallow of coffee and cleared her throat. "Well,
yes and no. I don't feel close to him, but I don't want him to die.

43

Mary, he's been an alcoholic all my life. He's tried Alcoholics' Anonymous several times. He stops drinkin' for a while, but he keeps fallin' off the wagon. I feel sorry for him. Mom has been dead for three years now. He has no one but me and a few of his AA buddies."

"Oh, I'm sorry to hear that. We have some alcoholics in our family, too. My ex-husband was an alcoholic. It's hard for the alcoholic. I really struggled with it, too."

The two women talked about alcoholism and their families for an hour.

Grace said, "I really have to go. I've got to get to work. I'm a waitress and my shift starts in a half hour."

As they approached the front door, Mary went to a bookshelf in her media center and pulled out an audio tape. "When you have time, you might want to listen to the story of Gert Behanna. It's quite a story. Gert was an alcoholic who recovered when she turned her life over to Jesus Christ."

"I'll be glad to listen," Grace said. "I must admit, I was hesitant in coming over. I was sure you were going to tell me about your conversion story. I'm not sure I was ready to hear it. Instead, you listened to my story."

"I will gladly tell you what happened to me, but I sensed that you were not ready to hear it today. When you're ready, I'll gladly tell you what God has done in my life. In the meantime, listen to Gert's story. You may want to play the tape several times. Please keep it. I got three copies when I attended a Field Seminary at our church several months ago."

"A Field Seminary?"

"Another story for another time."

When Grace got into her car, she glanced at the title on the tape, "God Isn't Dead" by Gert Behanna. She dropped the tape on the passenger seat and thought, *I'll have to listen to that sometime.*

When she got off work at midnight, she was "dead tired." It was a 45-minute drive home, and she wanted to be sure she stayed awake, so she popped the tape in her player.

The only reason that I have a right to stand up here and do what I do is because a man named Jesus Christ said to do this, Gert said. I'm no speaker; just a talker. In AA we call it "giving the pitch."

When I talk to an AA group I don't have to tell the people there what a miracle is. Every chair is occupied by a miracle. When I talk at churches, people think that miracles stopped with Lazarus. My life is a miracle.

When I tell my story, I have to speak about money, because I had so much of it. Money kept me from being aware of the poor. I was born to a group that thought they had a right to permanent and excessive privileges. We were separated from poor people.

Because I was rich, my excessive drinking, taking drugs, and the way I talked to people were all accepted. I know now all of these things were unacceptable, but they were accepted. My behavior was unacceptable, but it was accepted.

My father was brilliant; my mother beautiful. I was neither. How much this affected my later delinquency I don't know, but that it had something to do with it, I'm quite sure. My father was demanding. He expected me to go to the Sorbonne in Paris, become the U.S. Ambassador to England, and find a cure for cancer. The seeds of insecurity and shame, planted by these unreasonable demands, grew when I got my first divorce.

In my second marriage, after being a social drinker for years, I crossed the invisible line into alcoholism. Alcoholism is a mode of escapism. I wanted to escape from the life I had made for myself. Self pity was a way of life for me then. I could not blame myself because I wasn't willing to do anything about the problem and even if I had been willing to change, I didn't know what to do. I was a complete failure. I tried to escape into alcohol. Later I fled further from reality by using drugs.

After the third failed marriage, I tried suicide. I even failed in my attempt to take my life. A short time later a doctor said to me, "Gert, you are a very sick woman and there is nothing wrong with you. But make no mistake about it, you are a borderline case. Here are the names of two psychiatrists. See one of them."

45

I don't know where this came from, but I said it. "I don't need a psychiatrist. I need God." I didn't do anything about it, but I said it. The doctor who knew my spoiled behavior at the sanitarium where I was recuperating, replied, "God wouldn't hurt at all."

I went to New York and was dead drunk for six weeks. A friend invited me to come to her house and meet some friends of hers. "Why do you want me to meet them?" I asked.

"They were a lot like you and then they were converted," my friend said.

"Converted to what?" I asked.

"Converted to God," she said.

I went for the visit. How bad could it be to meet these people who called themselves Christians?

My first two Christians arrived. They ate their dinner. I drank mine. I bombarded them with questions. "So, you know God, do you? What is he like?"

After taking all my rude questions gracefully, the man finally said to me, "Gert, you do have problems, don't you? Why don't you turn them over to God?"

Stopped me cold. He meant it. Things that are meant can change us. "You mean turn my burdens over to God like I turn my suitcases over to a porter?"

"Something like that," he said.

He didn't try to correct me and tell me that our Lord is no porter. He let me have God as a porter. And he didn't quote Scripture. When you are talking to a Christian, it is okay to say, Leviticus 12:14, but when you are talking to a bum, you get nowhere by quoting the Bible.

When I got back home, I found a short note from this couple welcoming me home. That shocked me. They had seen me only one evening and I was totally drunk. They said that every morning they would sit down and pray for me. That rocked me. No one had ever prayed for me. They also said that they were sending me an article called "It's Never Too Late To Start Again" by Sam Shoemaker. They asked if I had time to read it. I had time. I rifled through the third class mail, found the article, and read it.

After twenty minutes or so, it was all over. It was more like a shower bath than anything. I prayed for the first time in my life, "I don't know who you are and I don't know anything about you, but if you are anywhere around, I surely could use your help." I felt accepted. I felt forgiven. I remember saying in my first prayer, "I will never take another drink again." And I haven't.

There was a prayer I had heard once. What was it? "Our Father...." Stopped me cold. Father. I who had a brilliant but demanding father now had a loving and accepting Father. Then I thought about all the people in the world who were my brothers and sisters. When I finished praying, I got up from my knees and headed for the phone.

I called my book man in Chicago and said, "I want two books: *The Joy of Cooking* and a Bible."

He said, "My God, what happened to you?"

I replied, "My God happened to me," and he had.

Next I wanted to find a church and a minister. I phoned an acquaintance of mine who was a Roman Catholic. I thought she might know of one.

"Do you want a go-getter or a man of God?" she asked.

"A man of God," I replied. Well, I got one. An Episcopal rector. You can warm your hands at the love that radiates from him. When I talked to him the first time, he told me about a man named Jesus who had died for a woman named Gert. He invited me to come to worship. That was the beginning.

Later I found that money belonged to God. The more I said, "Our Father," the more I realized that all this money I had didn't belong to me. It belonged to God, so I found ways to give it away. That was sixteen years ago. Since then, my life has been jammed packed. I'm 68 now and sometimes I get tired. I say to our Father, "Why don't you give me some time off?"

He replies, "You got onto this thing late, so just keep going."

My new life as a Christian boils down to two questions I ask myself daily:

1. Gert, how are you doing with Jesus Christ?
2. Is this for God or for Gert? If it is for God, I try to do it. If it's for Gert, I try not to do it. If I'm not sure, I wait.

I'm going to close now with a prayer. Don't close your eyes. Just listen.

Oh, Lord, I ain't what I oughta' be.
And, Lord, I ain't what I'm gonna' be.
But thanks, Lord.
I ain't what I used to be. Amen.

Grace found herself sitting in the car in front of her house, crying uncontrollably. This woman, Gert Behanna, was real. Grace couldn't believe in God, but she knew something had happened to her, something good.

At 7:00 a.m. the next morning she called Mary. "Where did you get that tape? I listened to it on the way home from work. When I got into bed, I couldn't sleep. I kept thinking about what Gert said. When you have time, I've got to talk to you."

"I've got time. Come on over."

"Gert really got to me," Grace said as Mary opened the door. "She's really somethin'."

"I thought you'd like her."

"Mary, I'm ready to hear what happened to you. I was afraid before. I thought you'd be preachin' at me and expect me to change. I just couldn't take some miracle story. Maybe I still can't, but I want to try. I'm sorry I put you off so long."

"No need to apologize. Do you have an hour or so?"

"Yes. I told Jake that I would be gone for a while."

"Jake?"

"Yeah. He's the man I live with. Nice guy. Doesn't believe in God or church or anything, but he's a nice guy."

"Okay," Mary said. "We can talk about Jake another time. Let me tell you about what God has done in my life.

"In some ways my story is unlike Gert's. I was not an alcoholic. She was. I was not divorced three times, only once. I was not rich. She was. I had a good, loving father. She had a major problem with her father. I had a good father. Although I thought

48

about it several times when my husband's alcoholism got to me, I never tried suicide. Gert tried to take her life.

"But in some other ways our stories are similar. My conversion, like Gert's, started with an awakening, moved to a commitment, and continued with Christian fellowship."

"Slow down," Grace said. "Let me think about what you just said. Awakening, commitment, and fellowship?"

"Yes," Mary said. "The awakening came two months after my divorce when my mother died. We were very close. We talked all the time. Her death left a big hole in my life. My husband and I hadn't gone to church very often — just once in a while on Christmas or Easter. At the time, I only knew a few people who worshiped regularly. I used to say, 'I'm as good as they are, so why should I go to church?'

"When my mother died, we needed a minister to bury her. I asked one of my Christian friends if she had anyone she'd recommend. She told me about Pastor Jeff Jackson. He's a little young, but he is a good man. He helped me a lot. He talked to me about alcoholism, divorce, death, and grief. He took my mother's funeral and then offered to continue to see me to help me with the adjustment. He even asked me if I might be interested in a grief group that his church had. I wasn't ready then, but later, after I worshiped a few times at Messiah Church I told Pastor Jeff I'd like to try it.

"It was in the grief group I met Sarah Williams. Sarah was a recent widow. She had a grandson who was always getting in trouble with the law. She told me the group really helped her overcome her worries and her grief. We became good friends. God used Sarah to help me discover what I have since come to call 'a hole in my soul.' "

"A hole in your soul?"

"Not a physical hole, but a real hole, nevertheless. Only God can fill that hole in the soul. You see, Grace, I had never been baptized. I had no religious training. My ex and I were good moral people, humanists, but there was no God in our lives. The alcoholism tested us beyond what we could handle. When I told Sarah about my lack of understanding and faith, she invited me to a

Pastor's class at church. She even attended the class with me. After class one night, Sarah and I went for coffee and a talk. It was there in the coffee shop that I realized what was happening to me. Sarah gave it a name. She called it 'an awakening.' "

"Like waking up from sleep?"

"Something like that. It was like I had been asleep to God all my life. I started to go to worship regularly and last Easter, I confessed Christ as Lord and Savior and was baptized."

"In front of the whole church? I could never do that."

"There were three of us adults from the Pastor's class who were baptized. Ten other adults joined the church by transfer. Four babies were baptized at the same time. It wasn't embarrassing at all."

"I could never do that," Grace repeated.

"Have you been baptized?"

"No, I don't think so. I guess I could ask my father. He would know, but, Mary, I just couldn't stand up in front of the church and be dunked in a tub of water."

"At our church we don't baptize people by dunking them under the water," Mary said. "The pastor just puts a few drops of water on people's heads."

"I'm sorry, but I am scared to death of being in front of a group. I could never do that."

"Don't rush things, Grace. Just take it a step at a time. Come to worship whenever you can. Sarah and I will look for you. You can sit with one of us. We will help you understand the liturgy and the sermons. Maybe the time will come for you to attend a Pastor's class sometime in the future. That's how you can learn about God, the Bible, and the church."

"I'll think about it, but I don't think you understand. Before I could do any of these things, I would have to change a lot of things in my life. I'm not good enough the way I am. I'd have to clean up my act."

There was a tear in Grace's eye as she spoke. *You don't know how low I've sunk with Jake — sex, booze, drugs, lying. I have to clean up my act, but I don't think I can.*

Mary put her arms around her. "Grace," she said, "we don't have to clean up our lives before God will accept us. We just have to come, warts and all, the way we are. God does the clean up work."

"I just can't believe that," Grace said. "I'm not acceptable."

"That's true for Sarah and for me and for all of us. Not one of us is acceptable to God. We are sinners. The miracle of grace is that Christ declares us accepted when we aren't acceptable. When you accept that you aren't acceptable but are accepted by God, you are on your way."

"That's pretty deep. I'll have to think about that one."

Questions For Personal Consideration And/Or Group Discussion

1. Like a lot of people, Grace Livingstone thinks she must clean up her life before she can come to God. What's wrong with this way of thinking?

2. What were the turning points in the story of Gert Behanna?

3. There are three stories at play in witnessing — your story, my story, and God's story. How did these three stories play out in the relationship between Grace and Mary?

4. How did the tape *God Isn't Dead* affect Grace's thinking?

5. What did the alcoholism of her father have to do with Grace's receptivity to what Gert Behanna said?

Digging Deeper

1. Alcoholism is a disease which some people say is genetic; others insist it is a learned behavior, and still others that it is a combination of these and other factors. The one consistent factor with alcoholics seems to be the practice of blaming others for what is wrong. The refusal to take responsibility for one's own behavior is present in many non-alcoholics as well as many alcoholics.

2. Feelings of inferiority often keep people from faith in God. These feelings produce false guilt, the feeling of being guilty when a person has not done something wrong. Real guilt comes from breaking God's laws, hurting God or people, and acting in selfish and self-centered ways. Real guilt is resolved by confession and forgiveness. False guilt is overcome by genuine acceptance and love.

3. What do you think about the outline of an adult turning to God: awakening, commitment, and fellowship?

4. Many Christians say that they were baptized as babies, raised in Christian homes, and believed in God since they were children. Isn't this just as good as being converted as adults?

Section Two:

Baptism Into The Kingdom Of God

Chapter Five

New Testament Baptism

Then Jesus came to them and said, "All authority in heaven and on earth has been given to me. Therefore go and make disciples of all nations, baptizing them in the name of the Father and of the Son and of the Holy Spirit, and teaching them to obey everything I have commanded you. And surely I am with you always, to the very end of the age." — Matthew 28:18-20

What did Jesus mean when he spoke these words? In order to answer that question, we need to look at the historical setting of the passage. Jesus was about to ascend into heaven when he gave this command. The words were the marching orders to the apostles who would see Jesus in the flesh no more. Notice, he starts by pointing out the authority by which he speaks his final words.

"All authority in heaven and earth ..." — that's a lot of authority. That's ultimate authority. That's God's authority. Authority means rights of authorship. Jesus is the author of the universe (see Colossians 1), the Word of creation (see John 1), through whom all things created were created. In other words, "Pay attention. These are your instructions, my final words of authority about what you are to do when I am gone."

"Make disciples." Disciples are followers. Disciples are under the authority of the Lord. Therefore, they try to be obedient believers. They repent when they fall short. They trust Christ as Lord and Savior. They follow the words and ways of Christ. Of course God does not expect the apostles or us to teach people about Christ or make disciples by our own power. Only God can make disciples, but Christians are called to witness for the Lord. The Holy Spirit will use that witness to make disciples.

"Baptizing them in the name of the Father, the Son, and the Holy Spirit." Baptism is the beginning of the Christian life. It is God's gift of the Holy Spirit. It is the way by which God makes people part of his kingdom family. The sacrament of Baptism is performed by limited human beings, but it is an act of God.

"I am with you always, to the very end of the age." Jesus assures us we are not alone as we witness for him. He reminds us of his presence to the very end of time.

Jesus is saying to the apostles and to us, "These are my instructions. Now get going for God." These instructions include baptizing people in the strong name of the Trinity: Father, Son, and Holy Spirit. These instructions bring us to the topic: Baptism Into The Kingdom.

People ask lots of questions about Baptism. We can't cover them all, but let's look at six frequently-asked questions.

1. Are there different kinds of baptism?[13]
2. Should infants be baptized?
3. Can you be baptized more than once?
4. Who can baptize?
5. Do you need to be baptized to be saved?
6. What do you do if you aren't sure you are baptized?

Are There Different Kinds Of Baptism?
At the time of Jesus there were at least three different kinds of baptism associated with Christianity. In order to understand what Jesus was commanding his followers to do, we need to understand the differences between these three.

First, there was proselyte baptism. Proselyte baptism was for Gentiles who wanted to become Jews. The ancient world was filled with all kinds of religions and sects. The uniqueness of the Jewish faith was its emphasis on monotheism and morality. Monotheism (as contrasted with idolatry) and morality (as contrasted with

56

immorality) attracted non-Jews to the faith. Some Gentiles wanted to become Jews. How did they achieve this purpose? They took instruction, were circumcised, and baptized. In Jesus' day, when Gentiles became Jews, they were given a special name. They were called "God-fearers." "God-fearers" were Gentiles who became Jews by faith.

For example, Cornelius, the Roman soldier who became a Christian, was first a God-fearer (Acts 10:2). He was a Gentile who chose to become a Jew by faith. Through the preaching of Peter, Cornelius was converted and baptized. Note that in Acts 10:34, Peter confesses: "I now realize how true it is that God does not show favoritism, but accepts men from every nation *who fear him* and do what is right."

Some scholars believe that many of the people who were initially converted to Christianity were God-fearers. The Jews thought of them as second-class citizens. When the apostles witnessed to them about Christ, they saw the completion of their spiritual journey in the gospel.

Proselyte baptism is not the same as Christian Baptism.[14] Cornelius and others had to be baptized in the name of the Trinity or in Jesus' name to become Christians.

Second, John the Baptist baptized Jews for repentance. His "hell, fire, and damnation" sermons on the banks of the river Jordan brought many Jews to revive their faith and receive baptism. But this baptism, like proselyte baptism before it, was not Christian Baptism.[15] John said so himself. "I baptize with water ... but among you stands one you do not know. He is the one who comes after me, the thong of whose sandals I am not worthy to untie ... Look, behold the Lamb of God who takes away the sin of the world ... The man on whom you see the Spirit come down and remain is he who will baptize with the Holy Spirit" (John 1:26-33. Also see Luke 3:16). In other words, the baptism of John, also called "a baptism of repentance," is not the same as the Baptism of Jesus.

Acts 18-19 verifies this distinction. Apollos, an early Christian preacher, had to be instructed in the truth about Baptism by Aquilla and Priscilla, Paul's disciples, "because he knew only the baptism of John" (Acts 18:25). We pick up the story in chapter 19 of Acts.

> *While Apollos was at Corinth, Paul took the road through the interior and arrived at Ephesus [today's Turkey]. There he found some disciples and asked them, "Did you receive the Holy Spirit when you believed?"*
> *They answered, "No, we have not even heard that there is a Holy Spirit."*
> *So Paul asked, "Then what baptism did you receive?"*
> *"John's baptism," they replied.*
> *Paul said, "John's baptism was a baptism of repentance. He told the people to believe in the one coming after him, that is, in Jesus. When Paul placed his hands on them, the Holy Spirit came upon them...."*
> — Acts 19:1-6

John's baptism was for the Jews who needed to repent in order to be ready for the coming of the Messiah. Jesus' Baptism was for Jews and Gentiles. It later came to be called a sacrament.

Third, the sacrament of Baptism, is for everyone. It is not primarily a matter of human beings choosing monotheism and morality over idolatry and immorality. It is not primarily a matter of seeing your wrongdoing, repenting, and choosing to be baptized. For adults it may seem that we are making these good choices, and achieving a new life, but Christian Baptism is not a matter of *achieving* anything. The sacrament of Baptism, for adults and children, is a matter of *receiving* something. As Luther says, "I cannot by my own reason or strength come to the Lord Jesus Christ, but the Holy Spirit...."

A sacrament is a sacred act of God for forgiveness containing an outward element and the word of God as instituted by Christ himself. In Baptism the outward element is water. The word of God is, "In the name of the Father and of the Son and of the Holy Spirit." That brings us to a second question people frequently ask.

58

Should Infants Be Baptized?

If Baptism is a sacrament of God, not a decision of human beings choosing God, then babies and children of all ages, as well as adults, may receive it. Baptism is an act of God, not an act of human beings. God does the choosing, not us.

In addition, if Baptism is the New Testament fulfillment of Old Testament circumcision, it is appropriate to baptize people of all ages, including children. Circumcision, the outward sign of the covenant God established with Abraham and Jews thereafter, was performed on Jewish boys, including Jesus, on the eighth day after birth.

In the third chapter of Galatians, Paul argues for the superiority of the New Covenant over the Old Covenant. He tries to show that circumcision, as given by God to Abraham, is now fulfilled in Baptism, the new covenant way for people to become God's children. He rises to heights of astonishment at what God has done in Jesus Christ through Baptism.

You are all sons of God through faith in Christ Jesus, for all of you who were baptized into Christ have clothed yourselves with Christ. There is neither Jew nor Greek, slave nor free, male nor female, for you are all one in Christ Jesus. If you belong to Christ, then you are Abraham's seed, and heirs according to the promise. — Galatians 3:26-29

This is a revolutionary concept. Baptism levels the playing field for all God's children. The Jews always considered Gentiles to be outsiders, even the ones who received proselyte baptism. Gentiles were hated people. Paul says by Baptism they are family. Slaves were inferior. Paul claims that baptized slaves are brothers and sisters. Females in Paul's time were viewed as property. By Baptism, Paul says they are members of the same kingdom as their male counterparts. Baptism is the new circumcision for Christians.

Acts 15 shows us the major controversy in the early church. The topic? Do Gentile converts have to be circumcised before they could be baptized and become Christians? We pick up the story in verse 1.

59

Some men came down from Judea to Antioch [where Paul was] and were teaching the brothers: "Unless you are circumcised, according to the custom taught by Moses, you cannot be saved." This brought Paul and Barnabas into sharp dispute and debate with them. So Paul and Barnabas were appointed, along with some other believers, to go up to Jerusalem to see the apostles and elders about this question.

There you have it. The hot topic at the first church convention was the relationship between Baptism and circumcision. The early Christians were deeply divided over this question. Paul had baptized Gentiles without first circumcising them. He was ridiculed by a party of the Pharisees who said, "The Gentiles must be circumcised and required to obey the law of Moses" (Acts 15:5).

Peter, one of the leaders in the early church, got to his feet and said, "Brothers, you know that some time ago God made a choice among you that the Gentiles might hear from my lips the message of the gospel and believe. God, who knows the heart, showed that he accepted them by giving the Holy Spirit to them, just as he did to us ... We believe it is through the grace of our Lord Jesus that we are saved, *just as they are*" (Acts 15:7-11).

The crowd at the church convention was silenced by Peter's words. Then Paul and Barnabas got up and told the stories of miraculous conversions and Baptisms God had worked among the Gentiles.

Finally, James, the brother of Jesus, now the head of the church in Jerusalem, took the floor and settled the matter.

It is my judgment ... that we should not make it difficult for the Gentiles who are turning to God. Instead we should write to them, telling them to abstain from food polluted by idols, from sexual immorality, from meat of strangled animals and from blood. For Moses has been preached in every city from earliest times and is read in the synagogues on every Sabbath.
— Acts 15:19-21

In other words, circumcision would not be required for Gentile converts to Christianity, because Baptism was the new entrance rite into the Christian faith. Circumcision was practiced on infants and adults. Why should Baptism be any different?

The *Westminster Dictionary Of The Bible* puts it this way:

> *Baptists contend that Baptism should be administered only to adult believers. The Church, however, from the earliest time has administered it also to children who have sponsors to care for their Christian nurture. It is certainly scriptural to do this to children of believers, since Paul expressly teaches (Galatians 3:15-29) that believers in Christ are under the gracious provisions of the covenant which God made with Abraham. Under that covenant circumcision was administered to children as a sign of their participation in the relation in which their parents stood to God. The children of Christian believers have therefore a similar right to the ordinance which has replaced circumcision.*[16]

If children can be baptized, then does that mean they automatically go to heaven? No. Baptism is like planting a seed. If the seed is not nurtured by sunshine and rain, it dies and never comes to harvest. In similar fashion, Baptism begins the process of salvation. Baptized children need nurture, love, education, and encouragement. Baptism makes them children of God, but not all children of God are obedient. What God has done by making us his children will never change, but what we do about what God has done is not permanent. If we turn away from God, we don't lose the fact that we have been baptized. Instead, we lose the benefits of having been baptized. That brings us to the third question people frequently ask.

Can A Person Be Baptized More Than Once?

Suppose a person is baptized in a Roman Catholic church as a baby and then as an adult decides to become a Lutheran. Should he be baptized again? Certainly not. Baptism makes you a child of God, not a Roman Catholic or a Lutheran.

Suppose a baby is baptized. At age eighteen, that person goes off to college, gets in with the wrong crowd, gets on drugs and into illicit sex, stops going to church and praying, and clearly leaves the care and nurture of God and the Christian community. Suppose at a later time when he marries and settles down, he realizes that his sinful ways have been wrong. He starts attending worship again. He starts praying again. Should he be baptized again?

NO! Why not? Because if a person knows what Baptism is — namely a sacred act of God — and is baptized a second time, he is saying that God didn't do it the first time. That's an insult to God. Since Baptism is an act of God, the problem is not that God didn't do it right the first time, but that the man in question has not responded properly to what God has done. Therefore he should repent for his erroneous ways and turn back to God's ways, but he should not be baptized a second time.

Those who believe in what is called "believers' Baptism" have no such limitations on multiple Baptisms. Since they believe Baptism to be a seal of the decision a person has made for Christ — not a sacrament — they consider a second or third Baptism just an outward sign of a repentant heart.

For Christians who believe Baptism to be a sacrament, repeating Baptism is inappropriate.

Who Can Baptize?

A fourth frequently asked question is, "Who can baptize?" In most cases, for good order, a pastor does the baptizing, but it may be done in emergencies by lay people.

Suppose a doctor says that a baby in a hospital may not live much longer. Suppose further that the family pastor is miles away from the hospital. Who can baptize the child? The answer is that any practicing Christian can baptize. A Christian doctor, nurse, friend or one of the parents can administer the sacrament of Baptism in these circumstances.

If someone other than a pastor does the Baptism, what two things do they need? One youngster in a confirmation class answered, "Water and the baby!" The correct answer is, "Water and the word." We assume the baby is there. Why water? It is commanded by Jesus. What word? The word Jesus gave to the apostles: "In the name of the Father, and of the Son, and of the Holy Spirit."

If the child survives, should the Baptism be repeated in a church by a pastor? Certainly not! When water and the word of God are combined, it is a genuine Baptism, a sacred act of God, which should never be repeated. The information about the child, the person who did the emergency Baptism, the date and place of the Baptism should all be recorded in a parish register of the church where the family members belong, but the Baptism itself should not be repeated.

We've covered answers to the first four frequently asked questions about Baptism. In the next section we'll tackle the remaining two frequently asked questions about Baptism:

1. Do you need to be baptized to be saved?
2. What do you do if you aren't sure you are baptized?

Grace Livingstone was listening to all this information about Baptism with great interest. During the coffee break at the end of the Pastor's class, she said to Sarah Williams, "I'm glad you invited me to come to this class. It was interesting. Pastor Jeff is a good teacher."

"Yes, he is," Sarah said with a smile, "but he doesn't have all the answers. Nobody does. When we get to heaven, we'll have to ask God a lot of questions."

"That's fine for you to say, but I don't know if I'm going to heaven. I checked with my father and he said as far as he knows, I've never been baptized."

She thought, *I don't deserve to go to heaven. I'm not worthy.*

Questions For Personal Consideration
And/Or Group Study

1. If you were Sarah Williams, what would you have said to Grace when she made the comment about not knowing if she was going to heaven?

2. Why do we baptize? (If you are in a group studying this matter, after discussing this question, turn to the Digging Deeper section and discuss the answer given there.)

3. What additional questions beyond the six mentioned in this chapter do you have about Baptism?

4. Baptism is not an "eternal life insurance policy." Do you agree or disagree?

5. What are some of the arguments by Baptists and others for adult Baptism *only*?

6. Read the nine baptismal stories in the book of Acts.
   - Acts 8:26-40 and Acts 9:1-19, which do not mention children
   - Acts 2:14-42, Acts 10:44-48, and Acts 19:1-10, which don't exclude children, but don't specifically mention them and
   - Acts 8:4-7, Acts 16:11-15, Acts 16:31-34, and Acts 18:5-11, all of which include infants and children

Digging Deeper

1. Why baptize? Good question. Let's begin by acknowledging the first creed of Christianity: "Jesus is Lord." If Christianity is not a democracy where we vote on what is right and wrong, but a monarchy with Jesus as the ruler and Lord, then the basic question we must always ask is, "What did Jesus say?" In this case, he taught that Baptism is necessary. We baptize because Jesus said to do it.

2. The baptism of Jesus by his cousin John the Baptist causes some confusion. John's baptism was a baptism of repentance. Jesus did not sin. Therefore he didn't need to repent. In fact, John protested, "I should not baptize you." Jesus replied that he should be baptized to "fulfill all righteousness." There are at least two possible explanations of these words:

   a. Jesus wanted to demonstrate that other Jews should be baptized by John to show the breaking in of the kingdom of God, and

   b. Jesus was beginning his identification with sinners that came to fullness on the cross when he died to pay their penalty for sin. In other words, he vicariously represented sinners, not only in his crucifixion, but from the beginning of his ministry, starting with his baptism by John. Paul said, "God made him [Jesus] who had no sin to be sin for us, so that in him we might become the righteousness of God" (2 Corinthians 5:21).

3. Should Baptism be by immersion only? About the mode of Baptism, *The Westminster Dictionary Of The Bible* says:

   Christians have differed, even from early times, as to the mode of Baptism. While the word is derived from a

65

verb, batizo, *which means, etymologically, to immerse, this does not prove that immersion was the mode always practiced, nor that it is necessary. In fact, instances occur where the word plainly does not mean immersion: (e.g. Luke 11:38, in A.V., wash; in R.V., bathe, and probably Mark 7:4). The Scriptures nowhere describe, much less prescribe, the mode. In post-apostolic times both immersion and affusion (sprinkling) were used.*[17]

4. Baptists, and some other denominations, teach that Baptism should be only for adults and only by immersion. They teach that Baptism is a seal of a person's confession of Christ as Lord and Savior. Repent first; then be baptized, they teach. They don't teach Baptism as a sacrament. Lutherans, Roman Catholics, and most mainline Protestant denominations teach that both adults and children may be baptized and that the mode of Baptism is not prescribed. Usually affusion (sprinkling) is the mode used in these churches.

5. The connection between Old Testament circumcision and New Testament Baptism is fascinating. Jewish boys were circumcised according to the covenant God made with Abraham (Genesis 17:1-12). Women were considered a part of the covenant family of God by virtue of being born into it or married into it. Male Gentiles were outsiders who if they wanted to become Jews had to be circumcised and baptized.

   The sacrament of Baptism retained the emphasis on God choosing us, but was inclusive. It was for males *and females,* Jews *and Gentiles,* children *and adults. In other words, anyone could become a Christian.*

Chapter Six

Do You Need To Be Baptized To Be Saved?

Jesus said, "No one can enter the kingdom of God unless he is born of water and the Spirit."
— John 3:5

Grace Livingstone was nervous about what the pastor would say about the necessity of being baptized. She was sitting next to Mary Anderson in the class. Sarah Williams who had attended the previous class with her was sick. Mary reached over and touched Grace's hand, as if to say, "Everything will be okay, Grace."

Pastor Jeff Jackson started the Pastor's class by reviewing the previous week's teachings about Baptism.

There were three primary kinds of baptism in the time of Jesus:

- proselyte baptism for Gentiles to become Jews,
- baptism of repentance taught by John the Baptist for Jews to renew their faith and anticipate the coming of the kingdom of God, and
- the sacrament of Baptism in the name of the Father and of the Son and of the Holy Spirit as instituted by Jesus himself.

Only the third kind is Christian Baptism. The first two were for adults who were called to make good decisions for God. The third was understood as a way in which God established a new covenant with his children, the new Israel, Christians. New Testament Baptism parallels Old Testament circumcision which was generally performed when a child was eight days old.

Infants and adults may receive the gift of grace in the sacrament of Baptism. In the Lutheran Church, the mode used is not prescribed. Jesus did not tell us how much water to use, only that we should use water combined with his word. When asked why we use water, we reply, "Jesus said so."

While any Christian can baptize in an emergency, usually the pastor does it in the church. Baptism is a once-and-forever act of God, so it should not be repeated, but it must be renewed. Luther said we must renew our Baptism daily by repentance. That brings me to the big question: "Do you need to be baptized to be saved?"

Let's start by looking at two important Bible verses. The first is John 3:5. Jesus said, "I tell you the truth, no one can enter the kingdom of God unless he is born of water and the Spirit." We understand that passage to refer to Baptism, the act of God by which he gives us the Holy Spirit. Notice, Jesus' strong emphasis on the necessity of Baptism. Jesus doesn't teach that Baptism is optional. "I tell you the truth," he says. He says this is the way into his kingdom.

In Mark 16:16 Jesus says, "Whoever believes and is baptized will be saved...." In most translations, this passage is footnoted because it may have been added at a later time to the rest of the Gospel of Mark.[18] For our purpose here we see that the passage says two things are necessary for salvation: faith and Baptism.

On the other hand, the second half of Mark 16:16 (sometimes called 16:16b) says, "But whoever does not believe will be condemned." In other words, two things are needed for salvation: 1) Baptism and 2) faith, but one thing condemns, namely not believing. While this may seem like an inconsistency at first, on closer examination we discover it is a profound paradox. A paradox is two seemingly opposite ideas, both of which are true, e.g. God is distant and close; Jesus is God and man.

The paradox we see here is on the one hand, we need both Baptism and faith for salvation, and on the other hand, one thing will separate us from God, the lack of faith. Of course, if we have faith in Jesus as Lord, we will do what he says. One of the commands Jesus gives is to be baptized.

Before we look further at the necessity of Baptism and the connection between Baptism and faith, let's examine the Roman Catholic answer to the question, "What happens to un-baptized people (including un-baptized babies) when they die?" Roman Catholic doctrine teaches that you can't get into Heaven without Baptism.

The Roman Catholic Church teaches that there are three levels in the afterlife: Heaven, Hell, and Purgatory. Heaven, it is taught, is where saints go directly upon death. Within this system, saints are defined as exceptional baptized believers who have done more good than evil in life. Some of their good works are "left over" and go into what is called "a treasury of merit." Other baptized believers can draw on this "treasury of merit" to shorten their time in Purgatory. Masses said for the dead are for this purpose.

Purgatory, it is taught, is a place where most baptized believers go. They will eventually go to Heaven, but first they must pay for the sins they have committed on earth. After a year or two or a hundred years of penalty, believers go on to Heaven. Time there can be shortened by people buying indulgences from the church or having masses said for the dead.

Of course, there is nothing in the Bible about Purgatory or a "treasury of merit." As a matter of fact, Martin Luther was so outspoken against this theological system, he protested vociferously against it. From these protests Protestantism got its name.

Un-baptized babies, good philosophers, and moral people who are not baptized, according to Roman Catholic doctrine, go to the top circle of Hell. Hell, it is taught, is a series of concentric circles descending to the headquarters of the Evil One. The top circle of Hell is called Limbo. Limbo, it is taught, is better than anything you have experienced in life, but there is no vision of God there. According to this teaching, the best chance un-baptized people have in the afterlife is Limbo.

Lutherans and other Protestants *do not* believe in Purgatory or Limbo. Quite the opposite! The Bible teaches salvation through Jesus Christ. The Bible says after we die there is only Heaven or Hell.

We have taken this side journey to show what one denomination has done to try to resolve the question of the necessity of Baptism and faith and what happens in eternity to those not baptized, according to this view.

In order to get at the question of what Lutherans and other Protestants teach about Baptism, faith, and eternity, it is helpful to consider the question, "Is there someone mentioned in the New Testament who was not baptized and yet clearly went to Heaven?" The answer is "Yes, there is." That person is the thief on the cross who by faith said to Jesus, "Remember me when you come into your kingdom." Jesus replied, "Today you shall be with me in Paradise."

No one got a ladder, crawled up on the cross, and baptized the believing thief who repented the last minute of his life, yet Jesus clearly told him he would go to Heaven that very day. What do we make of this? How can we reconcile this with John 3:5, Mark 16:16, and other Bible passages that imply the necessity of Baptism for salvation?

One way to view this problem is through the eyes of Hebrew thinking. It may help to compare Hebrew thinking to Greek thinking. The New Testament was written in Greek, but the writers were Jews. Greek thinking is definitive; Hebrew thinking descriptive. Jesus, a Jew, did not define God. Instead, he told parables about God. Greek thinking is built on the noun which is stable. Hebrew thinking is built on the verb, and is therefore action-oriented. If you want to know what God is like, look at what God did. Look at what Jesus did. From the cross Jesus announced the salvation of the thief. What does that tell us about God? In addition, two important distinctions between Greek and Hebrew thinking may help us wrestle with the question of the necessity of Baptism.

1. In Greek thinking, man (or woman) is in the center of things. In Hebrew thinking, God is at the center.
2. Greek thinking is speculative; Hebrew thinking practical. Concretely, in Hebrew thinking, God does his job and people are called to do their jobs. Who goes to Heaven is

God's business. Only God can decide the answer to that question.

It is *not* our job to decide who goes to Heaven and who goes to Hell. That's God's business, not ours. Our job is to do what Jesus told us to do, namely to preach, teach, and baptize in the name of the Father, Son, and Holy Spirit.

In other words, from our point of view, Baptism is necessary for salvation. Why? Jesus said so. On the other hand, as Lord, Jesus can make exceptions to his own rules, can't he? The thief on the cross is one such exception. Surely there are others, but it is speculation to determine who they are. We are called to the practical business of witnessing for the faith; not determining the outcome of those who have never heard the good news of Jesus or have never been baptized.

Grace was stunned by all this theology. She sat there motionless for the first minute of the coffee break. Her head was spinning. Mary asked her what she was thinking.

"I guess I'm thinking I should get baptized, but I'm afraid to do it."

"Can you tell me why you are afraid," Mary asked.

"I can't go up in front of all those people in church and get into a tank of water," she said. "I'm too embarrassed. I just couldn't do it."

"Grace, in our church we use just a few drops of water."

"I still can't do it in front of all those people. Walking down the aisle and all those eyes focused on me ... No way. People thinking, 'Why wasn't she baptized before now?' Standing there alone. I just couldn't do it."

"People wouldn't think that, but take your time. I'll pray for you."

Pastor Jeff finished the evening session with insights into what can be done if someone is not sure he or she is baptized.

71

What If You Aren't Sure You Are Baptized?

Some people aren't sure they are baptized. They say, "My parents are dead or don't remember. Other relatives are of no help. What should I do?"

Baptism is commanded by the Lord, so we try to follow that command, but in some cases, people just don't know if they have been baptized. God can save people without Baptism, but we should not expect him to do that since he has clearly told us that Baptism and faith are both necessary. What can be done?

In cases like this, there is something called "conditional Baptism" which can be practiced. In other words, if a person believes in Jesus Christ as Lord and Savior, but is unsure about whether or not he or she has been baptized, the pastor can baptize that person with the prefacing words, "In case you have not been baptized, I baptize you in the name of the Father and of the Son and of the Holy Spirit."

"I can't come next week," Grace told Mary. "I have to work."

"There will be other classes later," Mary said.

Three weeks after the second class on Baptism, Grace was at a worship service with Mary. When she didn't see Sarah at church, Grace asked Mary about her.

"She's sick, very sick," Mary said. "We don't know what's wrong, but she's sick to her stomach all the time and her skin is turning yellow. She's in the prayers of the church today."

"I'll pray for her too. She is such a good woman."

When people in the Pastor's class went forward to join the church, ten people transferred to Messiah Lutheran from other Lutheran churches. Five joined by what the pastor called "profession of faith." Four children of class members were baptized. In addition, two adults were baptized, one conditionally.

Later in the service, the new members and the rest of the congregation went forward to the front of the church for Holy Communion. Grace sat still as a rock.

"You can come forward and receive a blessing at the Communion rail," Mary said.

"I'm just not ready. I'm not even baptized."

I don't know if I'll ever be ready. It isn't just Baptism in front of all those people. It's also my lifestyle. These people just don't know the way I live. If they did, they wouldn't want me as a church member.

Questions For Personal Consideration And/Or Group Discussion

1. Do you know anyone like Grace Livingstone who is fearful of God and church? What are some of the possible reasons for these fears?

2. Is the distinction between Greek thinking which is speculative and Hebrew thinking which is practical helpful to you in regard to the question of who goes to Heaven?

3. What do you think about the Roman Catholic division of afterlife into three states: namely, Heaven, Hell, and Purgatory?

4. If Christ is the only way of salvation, what about people who have never heard the offer of salvation in his name? What about people of other religions? For some help with this question, see the Digging Deeper section for this chapter. Also see *I Believe; Help My Unbelief* (Ron Lavin, CSS Publishing Company, Lima, Ohio, 2001).

5. How can we encourage people to come to faith in Jesus Christ?

Digging Deeper

1. The New Testament teaches that Christ is the only way of salvation. For example, in John 14:6, Jesus says, "I am the way, the truth, and the life. No one comes to the Father except through me." Acts 4:10-12 reports Peter saying, "... Know this, you and all the people of Israel: It is by the name of Jesus Christ of Nazareth, whom you crucified but whom God raised from the dead, that this man stands before you healed. He is 'the stone you builders rejected, which has become the capstone.' Salvation is found in no one else, for there is no other name under heaven given to men by which we must be saved."

2. Saint Paul, the apostle, the greatest missionary of all time, says, "We proclaim him [Jesus], admonishing and teaching everyone with all wisdom, so that we may present everyone perfect in Christ. To this end I labor, struggling with all his energy, which so powerfully works in me" (Colossians 1:28-29).

   The word translated "perfect" in English in these verses comes from the Greek word *telos* which means whole or mature. One possible meaning here is that people who don't have faith in Jesus Christ are not yet whole or complete. That interpretation is supported by an understanding of the word "salvation." Salvation is not just what happens to us after death, but what happens in this life. Literally, salvation means "to be wide," or "spacious" or "to develop without hindrance."[19] In other words, in this life by faith in Jesus Christ we are given space, made more complete or whole, and given greater maturity, all in preparation for eternal life where we will be fully who we were created to be.

3. The Christian gets a foretaste of heavenly wholeness in the here and now. Those who are not baptized and do not have Christ as Lord and Savior do not have this foretaste of eternal

perfection. We evangelize to try to help everyone come to this foretaste of wholeness.

4. Baptism is a sacred act of God for forgiveness, containing an outward element (water) and the word of God ("In the name of the Father and of the Son and of the Holy Spirit"). The process of salvation is begun in us when God reaches across time and eternity and says, "You are my child. I have chosen you. You belong to me." That miracle of God's adoption into the faith family continues as we make personal confession of faith in Jesus Christ as Lord and Savior, at the time of confirmation and at other times.

5. We grow in Christ as we are nourished by the preaching of the word of God, receive Holy Communion, experience support from the fellowship of other believers, and use our spiritual gifts in the service of God and other people.

Chapter Seven

The Darkness And The Light

*The people walking in darkness have seen a great light;
on those living in the land of the shadow of death a
light has dawned.* — Isaiah 9:2

*The LORD is my light and my salvation — whom shall
I fear? The LORD is the stronghold of my life — of
whom shall I be afraid?* — Psalm 27:1

*... The message of the cross is foolishness to those who
are perishing, but to us who are being saved it is the
power of God.* — 1 Corinthians 1:18

*From that time on Jesus began to preach, "Repent, for
the kingdom of heaven is near."* — Matthew 4:17

These four Bible passages point us to the difference between
the people of darkness and the people of light. The also point us to
the way someone can cross from demonic darkness into the light
of the kingdom of God (or the kingdom of heaven, as Matthew's
Gospel puts it). In these passages we have bad news and good
news.

The Bad News

The Bible uses darkness as a way to describe people who do
not know God. There are two different kinds of people in the world:
those who know God and follow his ways, and those who do not

know God and do not follow his ways. The Bible calls these people "children of light" and "children of darkness."

In the first chapter of the Gospel of John, we read these words:

> *In the beginning was the Word, and the Word was with God, and the Word was God. He was with God in the beginning. Through him all things were made; without him nothing was made that has been made. In him was life, and that life was the light of men. The light shines in the darkness, but the darkness has not understood it.*　　　　　　　　　— John 1:1-5

Some translations read, "The darkness has not overcome it." One way or the other, the people of darkness just don't get what God has done for them by creating them in his image. They just don't get what Jesus Christ has done for them. The people of darkness don't recognize who Jesus is (John 1:10). They hate the light.

In Genesis the creation story is described in terms of darkness and light. There was darkness and a void and God said, "Let there be light and there was light."

> *In the beginning God created the heavens and the earth. Now the earth was formless and empty, darkness was over the surface of the deep, and the Spirit of God was hovering over the waters. And God said, Let there be light. God saw that the light was good, and he separated the light from the darkness. God called the light "day," and the darkness he called "night."*　　　　　　　　　— Genesis 1:1-5

The people of darkness refuse to acknowledge God as their Creator. They also refuse to recognize God as their Redeemer.

The powerful, dark powers of this world are evil. They work unbelief in the hearts of people. The children of light must be on guard at all times so that they do not succumb to the powers of darkness. The Great Deceiver is the god of this world. He has blinded the minds of unbelievers to the glory of Christ (2 Corinthians 4:4).

In this world there is a battle for people's minds and souls. It is the battle between believers and unbelievers. It is a battle between God and Satan. The Great Deceiver or Great Liar, as Satan is sometimes called, tries to lure us away from God. The Great Impostor, another name for Satan, makes promises of happiness and prosperity that will never be fulfilled. If we believe these lies and false promises, we end up in darkness.

Saint Paul warns against the powers of evil in Ephesians 6:12. He calls them "rulers of darkness, spiritual hosts of wickedness."

The bad news is that the powers of darkness are stronger than we are. The good news is that God is stronger than all the hosts of wickedness. The Bible teaches that ultimately God defeats the powers of darkness. Light overcomes darkness. We can be the recipients of God's victory over the Great Impostor. "God is light. In him is no darkness at all" (1 John 1:5). John 1:4 teaches that Jesus came to bring life and light to everyone who believes.

The bad news is we are sinners. The good news is Jesus died on the cross for sinners.

The Good News

All four of the passages cited earlier point to the way the good news overcomes the bad news. Isaiah 9:2 teaches that the people of darkness and shadows have seen a great light. Psalm 27:1 speaks of the Lord as my light, my life, and my stronghold. 1 Corinthians 1:18 tells us that the message of Jesus' crucifixion is foolishness to those who are perishing, but to those being saved, it is the power of God. In Matthew 4:17 Jesus tells the people of his time to repent for the kingdom of heaven is near.

Repentance is a way of life for the children of light. Being a part of the kingdom of heaven by Baptism and faith, we recognize our sins and bring them to the altar of God.

Those who are baptized and believe in Jesus as Lord and Savior receive the benefits of what Christ has done for them on the cross. The benefits include eternal life and light for this world and the next.

Jesus died for all, but those who refuse to believe are like a foolish man who is given a check for $1,000,000 but refuses to endorse it. The gift has been given, but they don't receive the benefits of it, because they refuse to sign it and make it their own.

Before Pastor Jeff could finish the main point of his sermon about the good news of the gospel and tell two stories of how people's lives have changed from darkness to light by God's grace, Grace Livingstone was on her feet and headed for the door. "I've got to go to the bathroom," she whispered to Mary who was sitting next to her. She did not return.

Grace cried all the way home. *They are always talking about repentance. How can repentance be a way of life? Why do I have to change? They are always talking about the importance of Baptism. Why do I have to be baptized? Why does there have to be bad news? Why can't we just have good news? What does God want me to do?*

Her eyes were red and swollen as she walked into her house. She tried to dry her tears before Jake, her live-in-boyfriend, noticed.

"What's the matter?" Jake asked as she entered the door. "I told you that church was nothing but trouble. You ought to quit and stay home with me on Sunday mornings, have a little sex, drink beer, and watch the football games on TV."

"You're right," Grace wept. "I just can't take it anymore. I'm through with all this church stuff. They keep talking about Baptism and belief. I'm not baptized and I don't even know anymore if I believe in God."

Later that day when Mary phoned her to ask if everything was okay, Grace lied. She said she had gotten sick at church that morning. In a way, it wasn't a lie. She was sick of hearing about sin, darkness, and the Great Deceiver. She was sick and tired of hearing about belief and Baptism. She was sick and tired of fighting with God.

Four weeks later, Mary phoned again. Grace was prepared. She would just tell Mary that her hours at the restaurant had been increased. She didn't have to explain that she had asked for more hours. She had to work Sunday mornings. She couldn't attend church anymore. *That should end all this struggle about God and church*, she thought.

"Grace, I'm sorry to tell you this, but our friend Sarah Williams just died. It was pancreatic cancer. I thought you might want to know."

Questions For Personal Consideration
And/Or Group Discussion

1. Why do pastors preach and teach both the law (bad news) and the gospel (good news)?

2. What are the dangers of preaching and teaching both the law and the gospel?

3. What would happen if preaching and teaching the bad news about sin, darkness, and the Great Deceiver were eliminated?

4. How do stories of the good news of people moving from the kingdom of darkness to the kingdom of light help other people?

5. How would you describe

   a. the bad news?_____
   _____

   b. the good news? _____
   _____

6. Do you agree or disagree with the statement: "Preaching should afflict the comfortable and comfort the afflicted"?

Digging Deeper

1. There is a difference between guilt and false guilt. Guilt comes from doing or thinking in ways that are contrary to God's law. Guilt comes from hurting God and people. Guilt comes from self-centered actions and thoughts. Guilt is relieved by repentance and forgiveness.

    On the other hand, false guilt feels just as bad as real guilt, but its source is different. False guilt comes from feelings of inferiority. People feel false guilt, even when they haven't done something wrong. False guilt is not relieved by repentance and forgiveness, but by acceptance and love.

    Grace Livingstone, as described in this book, has a dangerous mixture of both guilt and false guilt.

2. Grace Livingstone has massive inferiority feelings. These feelings got "hooked" by the first part of Pastor Jeff's sermon on bad news. Because so many people, like Grace, have false guilt because of feelings of inferiority, should Pastor Jeff have skipped over the bad news of sin, darkness, and the Great Deceiver?

3. One possible approach to preaching and teaching both the law and the gospel might be called "the bookends" approach where we start and end with the good news.
    a. Good news about God's love and grace
    b. Bad news of our sinfulness and need for love and grace
    c. Good news about God's love and grace

Chapter Eight

Baptized Into His Death

... Don't you know that all of us who were baptized into Christ Jesus were baptized into his death? We were therefore buried with him through Baptism into death in order that just as Christ was raised from the dead through the glory of the Father, we too may live a new life.   — Romans 6:3-4

Christ's death and resurrection are intricately interwoven with the death and resurrection of his people. God is a God of grace, who gives us much more than we deserve.

> Justice means getting what we deserve.
> Mercy means not getting what we deserve.
> Grace means getting what we do not deserve.

At death, justice means we get what we deserve. Death is a part of our fallen state. "The wages of sin is death" (Romans 6:23a).

At death, God's mercy means that we don't get what we deserve. We don't have to pay the wages of sin. Christ, by his death on the cross has taken the punishment for all of us. We deserve punishment. We receive mercy. "... Like the rest [of the disobedient sinners], we were by nature objects of wrath. But because of his great love for us, God, *who is rich in mercy*, made us alive with Christ even when we were dead in transgressions ..." (Ephesians 2:4-5).

83

Most important, at death, grace is at work. We get what we do not deserve. Saint Paul puts it this way, "... It is by *grace* you have been saved, through faith — and this not from yourselves, it is a gift of God — not of works, so that no one can boast" (Ephesians 2:8-9). "The wages of sin is death, but the gift of God is eternal life in Christ Jesus our Lord" (Romans 6:23). Eternal life is a gift of God's grace.

When we die, we receive what we do not deserve — eternal life. We receive this gift not because we are good, but because God is good. God's goodness is supremely expressed by the action of Christ dying for us on the cross. "... God so loved the world that he gave his one and only Son, that whoever believes in him shall not perish but have eternal life" (John 3:16).

Christians, like other people, die physically, but we have the promise of Christ that we will live again because of what he has done for us. Sarah Williams was a sinner redeemed by the grace of God in Christ. She was a saved sinner. She was a forgiven sinner. She was a saint.

As Saint Paul said, "By Baptism we are buried with Christ in his death so that like him we too might be raised and given new life."

After the funeral at Messiah Church, there was a reception in the Fellowship Hall. Grace, who had sworn that she would never go back to church, was there. "I liked Pastor Jeff's sermon about Sarah," she said to Mary Anderson. "Sarah Williams was a good Christian woman. She was always kind and loving to me."

"Yes, she was one of the best," Mary replied.

"What did the pastor mean by saying that we all are sinners deserving punishment for our sins?"

"Sarah, like all of us, was a sinner. She, like all of us, needed Christ's mercy for forgiveness and grace for eternal life."

"That's hard for me to accept. She was such a good person. Isn't heaven a reward for people like Sarah who are truly good?"

"No. We are saved only by the grace of God in Jesus Christ. None of us deserves heaven. Heaven is not a reward for good people. Heaven is a joyous reunion with God who by grace invites us to come to him."

"Grace?"

"Grace. As the pastor said, 'Grace means getting what we do not deserve.' "

I just don't get it, Grace screamed in her mind. *I just don't understand you Christians. You tell us to be good, but then turn around and say that we are not rewarded for being good. God, what's it all about?*

Questions For Personal Consideration And/Or Group Discussion

1. Why is salvation by grace alone so hard for outsiders to understand?

2. What would you say to Grace if she raised her questions with you?

3. What brought Grace to Sarah's funeral service after she vowed never to return to the church?

4. If you are in a group, discuss justice, mercy, and grace.

5. Why should we be good if good works are not rewarded in heaven?

Digging Deeper

1. Read Ephesians 2:4-9. What does this passage mean?

2. Read Romans 1:16-17. What does this passage mean?

3. Martin Luther talked of the joyous exchange of Christ's suffering and death for our sins. What does this mean?

4. Other uses of the term "baptism."
   a. Baptism for the dead. In 1 Corinthians 15:29, Saint Paul uses this confusing and difficult phrase. It may mean being baptized at the graves of martyrs (sacred ground) with the cloud of witnesses around. It may mean "on behalf of" (e.g. being baptized because of the witness of a loved one who has died, thus showing affection and respect for the faith of the one who has died). It may mean "to fill the vacant places in the Church left by those who have died." It probably refers to vicarious Baptism, i.e. being baptized for a person who was under Christian instruction, but died before he or she could be baptized.[20]

   A good principle for exegesis is to interpret difficult passages like this one in the light of clear passages.

   b. Baptism of the Holy Spirit. Pentecostals use this term to refer to "speaking in tongues." They teach three baptisms: 1) conversion and confession of Christ as Savior, 2) Water baptism to seal your confession, and 3) baptism of the Holy Spirit (speaking in tongues). They teach that water baptism does not give the Holy Spirit. Lutherans and other Christians teach that the sacrament of Holy Baptism with water and the word gives the Holy Spirit.

Section Three:

The Kingdom
Eucharist

Chapter Nine

Old Testament Passover And New Testament Sacrament

... I received from the Lord what I also passed to you: The Lord Jesus, on the night he was betrayed, took bread, and when he had given thanks, he broke it and said, "This is my body, which is for you; do this in remembrance of me." In the same way, after supper he took the cup, saying, "This cup is the new covenant in my blood; do this, whenever you drink it, in remembrance of me." For whenever you eat this bread and drink this cup, you proclaim the Lord's death until he comes.   — 1 Corinthians 11:23-26*

Baptism is the first sacrament. A sacrament is a sacred act of God for forgiveness of sins as instituted by Jesus Christ.

The second sacrament is called the Lord's Supper or the Last Supper because it was the last meal of our Lord on earth. It is also called Holy Communion because in it God gives us union with him and with one another. In addition, it is called the Sacrament because in, through, and under the bread and wine, God is acting to give us the body and blood of our Lord Jesus Christ.

Alternatively, the Lord's Supper is called the Eucharist. Eucharist means thanksgiving. When we celebrate the Eucharist, we are giving thanks for the precious gift of Jesus Christ himself.

Before we look further at the implications of these various titles, let's examine the Old Testament Passover. Jesus was celebrating the

Jewish Passover when he said, "Take, eat, this is my body ... This cup is the new testament in my blood."

The Passover

Moses had been called by God to free the Hebrews from Egyptian bondage. He told Pharaoh the LORD said, "Let my people go." Pharaoh refused to heed the command to set the enslaved Hebrews free. Plagues were sent upon Egypt to show God's wrath and judgment on Pharaoh for his stubbornness. The last plague was the slaying of the firstborn sons of Egypt.

Moses told the Hebrews to mark their doorposts with the blood of a lamb so that the angel of death would pass over the Hebrew houses. The firstborn sons of Egypt, including Pharaoh's firstborn son, were the casualties. Pharaoh agreed to let the Hebrew people go. Thereafter, to this day, the Jews celebrate the Passover meal in remembrance of freedom from bondage. It is a long celebration meal of several hours. It involves children who ask questions to help them learn the history and tradition of their people. It is a highly symbolic meal, repeated year after year, binding the Jews to one another and to God.

At Passover, the Jews eat lamb to remember the blood of the lambs on the doorposts which had saved their ancestors from death. They eat bitter herbs to remember the bitterness of slavery. They eat something sweet to remember the promise of the land to which Moses led them. Passover is the celebration of deliverance from bondage in Egypt and freedom in the Promised Land.

Wine and unleavened bread are two of the most important elements of the Passover meal. The grape vine is the symbol of Israel. Wine, the drink of the Passover, reminds the Jews of their national heritage and spiritual prosperity under God. They drink wine several times during the Passover liturgy as an important reminder of who they are. Many stories are told to enforce the heritage of the people of God.

Unleavened bread is used for Passover because the Jews had to leave Egypt in a hurry. They didn't have time to let the bread dough rise, so they packed loaves of unleavened bread for the long trip. Thereafter, year after year unleavened bread was used in the

Passover meal to remind the Jews of their hurried departure from the land of bondage. At Passover, someone (usually a child) asks, "Why do we eat unleavened bread tonight?" The story of the last meal in Egypt is told with great delight and emphasis on how God led his people out of slavery across the desert to the Promised Land.

When the Jews ran out of food on the long journey, God sent them bread from heaven. This bread from heaven is called manna. Literally, manna means "What is it?" which is what the people said when they discovered this bread on the ground and were told that they must gather it fresh each morning.

Jesus, a Jew, celebrated Passover with his disciples in the upper room of John Mark's house. He did this the night before he was crucified.

The Kingdom Eucharist

At the Passover celebration in Jerusalem, Jesus used the traditional elements of the Passover meal, including unleavened bread and wine. "Remember your heritage of freedom from bondage," he was saying to his followers. Then he added a sacramental emphasis for the future. "Take and eat; this is my body," he said. "... This is my blood of the covenant, which is poured out for many for the forgiveness of sins. I tell you, I will not drink of this fruit of the vine from now on until that day when I drink it anew with you in my Father's kingdom" (Matthew 26:26-29).

This is the Lord's Supper because Jesus initiated it. This is the Last Supper because it was Jesus' last meal on earth. This is Holy Communion because through the elements we are joined to the Lord and one another. This is the Sacrament because it is a sacred act of God for forgiveness. This is the kingdom Eucharist because it points beyond itself to the end of the world when the fullness of the kingdom will come. We are called to rejoice in this promise.

Christians, like the Jews before them, see this holy meal as a reminder of their heritage and an invitation to take heart for the future. Christians, like the Jews before them, remember the blood of the lamb on the doorpost, but for Christians it is the blood of the Lamb of God on the cross which is recalled when they eat and

91

drink the elements of this new covenant (testament) meal. Like the Jews before them, Christians use unleavened bread and wine. (See Digging Deeper for exceptions to wine.)

In contradiction to God's intended unity, in some ways Christians have been divided in their interpretations of the meaning of this sacred meal. The good news is that some of the distinctions historically made by different groups are breaking down, in a new convergence of understanding, but the fact remains that different Christians have different understandings of the Eucharist. Below find a chart of the main historical interpretations of Holy Communion as practiced by three different groups of Christians: Roman Catholics, Reformed Protestants, and Lutherans.

Group	What they teach
1. Roman Catholics Transubstantiation	We receive only the body and blood of Christ, not bread and wine. The elements are once and forever transformed into the body and blood of Christ. Only a priest can consecrate the elements. Only a priest may take both elements (Unevenly practiced today. Some churches serve both elements to all the people.) The elements remain the body and blood of Christ after the Mass. The Lord's Supper is a sacrament.
2. Reformed Protestants Symbolism	We receive only bread and wine, not the body and blood of Christ. What is received is just a symbol or remembrance of what happened at the Last Supper. Generally grape juice is used instead of wine.

3. Lutherans	We receive the body and blood of
Real Presence	Christ in, through, and under the
	elements of bread and wine.
	The Lord's Supper is a sacrament.
	We don't know *how* but we believe
	that we receive Christ in the
	Lord's Supper.

Lutherans teach that the Roman Catholics are right in what they affirm about Christ's presence, but wrong in what they deny. In the Lord's Supper, Lutherans believe we receive the body and blood of the Lord, *and* bread and wine. Lutherans teach that the Reformed Protestants are right in what they affirm about remembering, but wrong in what they deny about the real presence. In the Lord's Supper, Lutherans believe we receive bread and wine *and* the body and blood of Christ. It is a remembrance, but it is more.

When asked why Lutherans place such a strong emphasis on the Lord's Supper, the answer is we believe Jesus put that strong emphasis on it. When asked why Lutherans believe that Jesus is really present in the Lord's Supper, the best reply is, "Jesus said so. We don't attempt to explain how it is possible, but we believe we receive what Jesus said we would receive."

What difference does it make that Christians receive the Lord's Supper often? Since we receive forgiveness through the Sacrament, it is important to receive it often. Since Jesus promised to be present, we should be present. Since Jesus mentions the Lord's Supper and the coming kingdom, we believe receiving him through the elements of bread and wine gives us a foretaste of the Great Banquet at the end of time.

In addition, consider the mystical communion of all the saints of God, both in the Church militant (on earth) and the Church triumphant (in heaven). In the Lord's Supper we commune with God. We also commune with other Christians of all denominations in all places on the earth. In Holy Communion we even commune with those Christians who have died and are now in the Church Triumphant.

Holy Communion is truly a celebration of the kingdom Eucharist. The kingdom of God is God's rule over us. As we come under the lordship of God, our lives make sense and we are renewed by God's forgiveness. In Holy Communion we all come as sinners, kneeling before God, with no one better than anyone else. Baptized believers are given a preview of coming attractions. They get a preview of God who rules over all for our own good. We give thanks for what God will do, but we also give thanks for what God has done and is doing. The past, present, and future are all wrapped up in one when the pastor says, "The body and blood of Christ, given and shed for you."

"Wow," Grace said to her friend Mary. "That was quite a Pastor's class session. Pastor Jeff really laid it out there today. I told you I didn't want to come, but I'm glad you persisted. As I told you, I had decided I wouldn't ever be coming back to church. I felt I couldn't handle all the things taught here, but a little light is beginning to get through. It's all gift, isn't it? God does for us what we can't do for ourselves."

"God is working in your life, Grace. It's called 'the awakening.'"

"I don't know about that. Jake told me I'm a damned fool for going back to church, but I listened again to that tape you gave me. That helped. Sarah's funeral helped, too. She was such a fine Christian lady. I wish my family had been more like her."

"Grace, you said your father is sick and you are concerned about him. Do you want to ask the pastor to make a visit on him? Maybe he could even bring Holy Communion to him."

"I'll have to ask Dad if that's okay." *Dear God, give me the right words.*

Questions For Personal Consideration
And/Or Group Discussion

1. Is the chart on the distinctions between the three different churches on the Lord's Supper helpful or does it draw too much attention to the differences and not show enough of what we have in common as Christians?

2. What are some of the churches that are generally listed under the Reformed Protestant label?

3. Episcopalians and Lutherans generally agree on the meaning of the Lord's Supper as being both the body and blood of Christ and the bread and wine. What differences remain between these two groups?

4. Can (should) a Lutheran receive Holy Communion in a Roman Catholic church? Why or why not?

5. Can (should) a Lutheran receive Holy Communion in another Protestant church? Why or why not?

6. Under what circumstances can a non-Lutheran receive the Lord's Supper in a Lutheran church?

7. The question about the appropriate age at which children should receive Communion has been hotly debated in recent years. At what age or under what conditions do children receive Communion in your congregation?

8. What should an unbaptized person like Grace Livingstone do when Communion is celebrated and she is present?

Digging Deeper

1. Different denominations and different pastors of the same denomination have different opinions about the appropriate age for Communion. Some churches today even commune baptized infants. On the other hand, some churches offer Communion only to those who have completed confirmation. While this may cause confusion for some people, the positive side of the situation today is that people have many choices regarding which church they will join. One of the factors in this decision is the practice of Holy Communion.

2. The term "Holy Eucharist" is generally used by Catholics, Episcopalians, and Lutherans. By tying the Eucharist to the kingdom of God, we connect this sacrament to the Great Banquet to which Jesus often pointed.

3. In the Apostles' Creed, we speak of the Church as "the communion of the saints." Both the living and the dead saints (forgiven sinners) are in communion with God and one another. Communion between the living and the dead saints can be helpful to those who have un-reconciled differences with loved ones who have died before forgiveness can be offered or accepted.

4. Jesus used wine in the institution of the Lord's Supper. After all, it was a Passover celebration. Jews use wine, not grape juice, for Passover. In addition, there was no refrigeration in Jesus' day, so the fruit of the vine, put into wineskins would turn into wine in a short time in the hot Palestinian sun. In

many churches today, grape juice is offered as an option for alcoholics, pregnant women, people on certain medications, and others who prefer grape juice for personal reasons.

5. Can we take Communion in an unworthy way? 1 Corinthians 11:27-29 says: "... Whoever eats the bread or drinks the cup of the Lord in an unworthy manner will be guilty of sinning against the body and blood of the Lord. A man ought to examine himself before he eats of the bread and drinks of the cup. For anyone who eats and drinks without recognizing the body of the Lord eats and drinks judgment on himself."

   Biblical scholar William Barclay says, "The unworthiness consisted in the fact that the man who did so did 'not discern the Lord's body.' " That phrase can equally well mean two things; and each is so real and so important that it is quite likely that both are intended.

   a. It may mean that the man who eats and drinks unworthily does not realize what the sacred symbols mean. It may mean that he eats and drinks with no reverence and no sense of the love that these symbols stand for or the obligation that is laid upon him.

   b. It may also mean this. The phrase *the body of Christ* again and again stands for the Church ... It may mean that unworthiness comes from hatred, bitterness, contempt against his brother man, as he comes to the Table of our Lord.[21]

   Consider this possibility. The point of the Eucharist is celebration of the forgiveness of sins. We are called to repent and thus receive the forgiveness of sins. Therefore it is important as we approach Communion to repent for our sins. Persons who are unworthy of receiving Communion are those who think they are worthy and need no repentance. Those who are worthy are those who know they are unworthy sinners and thus repent.

Chapter Ten

The Sacrament And The Prodigal

Now the tax collectors and "sinners" were all gathering around to hear him. But the Pharisees and the teachers of the law muttered, "This man welcomes sinners and eats with them...."

Jesus (said): "There was a man who had two sons. The younger one said to his father, 'Father, give me my share of the estate.' So he divided his property between them.

"Not long after that, the younger son got together all he had, set off for a distant country and there squandered his wealth in wild living. After he had spent everything, there was a severe famine in that whole country, and he began to be in need. So he went and hired himself out to a citizen of that country, who sent him to his fields to feed pigs. He longed to fill his stomach with the pods that the pigs were eating, but no one gave him anything.

"When he came to his senses, he said, 'How many of my father's hired men have food to spare, and here I am starving to death! I will set out and go back to my father and say to him: Father, I have sinned against heaven and against you. I am no longer worthy to be called your son; make me like one of your hired men.' So he got up and went to his father.

"But while he was still a long way off, his father saw him and was filled with compassion for him; he ran to his son, threw his arms around him and kissed him.

"The son said to him, 'Father, I have sinned against heaven and against you. I am no longer worthy to be called your son.'

"But the father said to his servants, 'Quick! Bring the best robe and put it on him. Put a ring on his finger and sandals on his feet. Bring the fattened calf and kill it. Let's have a feast and celebrate. For this son of mine was dead and is alive again; he was lost and is found.' So they began to celebrate.

"Meanwhile, the older son was in the field. When he came near the house, he heard music and dancing. So he called one of the servants and asked him what was going on. 'Your brother has come,' he replied, 'and your father has killed the fattened calf because he has him back safe and sound.'

"The older brother became angry and refused to go in. So his father went out and pleaded with him. But he answered his father, 'Look! All these years I've been slaving for you and never disobeyed your orders. Yet you never gave me even a young goat so I could celebrate with my friends. But when this son of yours who has squandered your property with prostitutes comes home, you kill the fattened calf for him!'

" 'My son,' the father said, 'you are always with me, and everything I have is yours. But we had to celebrate and be glad, because this brother of yours was dead and is alive; he was lost and is found.' "

— Luke 15:1-2, 11-32

"Dad," Grace said, "my friend Mary Anderson said it would be a good idea for me to ask you if you would like to have the pastor come and see you here in the your home. You really need some help, you know." She said it with conviction.

Her father, surprised by his daughter's strength, hedged. "It's been so long since I attended church. I don't know. I just don't know. Maybe if I can straighten up my attitude, forgive some people who have hurt me, and continue to stay on the wagon for a few more months — maybe then the pastor could come. I'm glad you are going to church, but I'm just too old to start over again with

God. I'm just not good enough. You, of all people, know that. I haven't exactly led an exemplary life. I'll think about it, but I just don't think it's right. Maybe later."

Grace didn't want to frighten her father, but she felt she just had to say it. "Dad," she choked on the word. "Dad," she started again, "I'm not surprised by what you said, but there may not be much more time 'later.'"

The next Sunday morning Grace met Mary outside the church. "How did it go?" Mary asked.

"He said, 'No.' Actually he said, 'Maybe later,' but that means 'No,'" she said sharply. "I knew he'd say that. All his life it's been 'Later.' Later he'd stop drinking. Later, he'd start treating me with some respect. Later, he'd start treating mom like a woman should be treated. Later, later, later. Well, there is no later for mom. She's dead and gone. She never had a real husband who cared for her. I'm tired of hearing 'Later.'"

Mary didn't comment on Grace's father's response. She just put her arm around Grace. "God will help you," she whispered as they walked into church.

Pastor Jeff was excited about the text on which he was preaching that morning. "As far as I'm concerned, it is the best story anyone has ever told. It is a story about the heart of God. It is a story about grace," he said softly. Then he spoke with force.

Justice means we get what we deserve. Justice is at play in this story. We all know what the prodigal son deserves. Punishment. The elder son is right, isn't he? The younger son has disappointed and disobeyed his father. He should be punished, shouldn't he?

Mercy means that we don't get what we deserve. Mercy is at play in this story. We feel great relief when God is willing to forgive his son and not punish him for what he has done. Maybe that means that God will give us mercy, too. Maybe he won't punish us the way we deserve to be punished.

Best of all, grace is at play here. That's the scandal in the story. That's what upset the elder son. That's what upset the Pharisees and the teachers of the law who heard the story. That's what caused them to mutter, "This man welcomes sinners and eats with them." That's what kept the elder son outside the party, isn't it? He couldn't tolerate the father's willingness to give his sinful brother what he in no way deserved.

Give him a year or two to prove himself, the elder son must have thought. *What is to keep him from doing the same thing again? Give him the ring of ownership again? Throw a party for him? No way! He'll take advantage of you. You'll see. Father, you are blind as a bat. You just don't know what kind of a man your son is. You'll see! You'll see! No way can I come to a party for a man like him. No way! No way! What about me? You've never done anything like this for me! And I have done all the right things. All the right things.*

And we might very well be thinking the same thing. There is a scandal here. Grace flies in the face of reason and justice. Grace defies common sense. Grace means that we get what we in no way deserve. If you aren't sure yet, confer with the prodigal himself. He isn't expecting anything but maybe the possibility he can become a servant. He has his speech ready, "I don't deserve anything ... but maybe, Father, I could just work as a slave for a little while...." He is shocked. He is disturbed. He is amazed. *The ring on my finger? A party for me? No way! No way! I don't deserve it....*

But the boy never gets to make his speech. The father takes over. Grace dominates the scene. Generosity beyond belief! Amazing grace. Saving grace.

The pastor choked on the words. He was preaching beyond his capacity and he knew it. He was out of control and something, Someone, was speaking through him. He was speaking, yes, but he was also listening as if Someone else was speaking. He was preaching the word of grace, which is beyond description. *Lord, help me,* he prayed.

Grace Livingstone was stunned. She had never heard anything like this before. She froze with fright. How could this be? *"This is not what I thought God was like. It can't be true. It just can't."*

Mary, noticing that Grace was stiff as a board, tense, and afraid, put her hand on Grace's. "It's okay," she said. "God loves you. Hold on."

"And the feast?" the pastor pondered. "It is a banquet for the undeserving. It is a party for sinners, a foretaste of the feast to come. If you don't think you are a sinner, you won't see your need to come; you won't repent. Or if you come, you won't get the benefits of what God gives. But to sinners who come home, there is grace.

"Grace. Pure grace. For you in Holy Communion. Come. Listen to the words again. 'For you. Given and shed for you.' Come. You and I are prodigals, fresh from a journey away from our Father. Undeserving. Needy. Prodigals. But the Father is waiting. He welcomes us with open arms, saying, 'Let's have a banquet.' Come.

"Here there is manna, bread from heaven, kingdom bread, the wonder bread of grace. 'The body of Christ for you.' Come. Taste it again for the first time. Come."

Something was forming in Grace's mind. It was something new. She had always been afraid of commitment. She couldn't trust men. She was afraid to trust anyone, even God. *Could God actually accept me?* She mused. *No way!* a voice within her screamed. But there was another voice. *Grace, come unto me. I am the good shepherd. I will take care of you. I love you. Come home.*

Grace put her hands over her face and held it. Her head hurt. *Two voices. Am I going crazy? What am I to do? God, help me. I can't handle this. I have had to fight all my life. God, I don't want to fight with you anymore.*

"Grace, are you okay?" Mary's voice broke in.

"Just a headache." *What a headache.*

Grace, I love you. Come home.

When the usher came to the aisle where Grace and Mary were seated to usher them forward for Communion, Grace bolted for the side door, Mary right after her.

Questions For Personal Consideration
And/Or Group Study

1. What was Grace's problem?

2. If you were Mary, what would you say to Grace?

3. What are the implications of the story from Luke 15 for Grace Livingstone?

4. What are the implications for Grace's father?

5. What connection do you make between the Pharisees and teachers of the law at the beginning of the story and the elder son at the end of the story?

6. The father in Jesus' story went out to both of his sons. One, though befuddled, came to the party. The other, filled with resentments, refused to come to the banquet. He stood out by the barn muttering. What do you make of this?

7. Reversals are important in all story telling. What reversals take place in this story?

Digging Deeper

1. This story should not be called "The Story Of The Prodigal Son," but "The Story Of The Waiting Father."[22] The story is not really about the son who repents, but about the father who is willing to forgive. The Pharisees and teachers of the law could understand if a sinner turned away from sins and repented. They would agree that God could forgive such a person. What they found thoroughly intolerable was what looked like a permissive God who didn't take sin seriously. Was Jesus unmindful of how offended God is when we sin? Wouldn't people take advantage of that kind of divine generosity? How can God restore to full family acceptance, people who come home after deserting him? Didn't the father understand that law and justice are necessary for an ordered society? The law is supposed to break our pride and convict us of our wrongdoing, isn't it?

2. What bothered the Pharisees, the teachers of the law, and the elder son? The scandal of divine generosity is beyond our wildest dreams. It was grace they could not or would not stomach. Some people today have the same problem.

3. If, as Jesus is saying, grace comes before as well as after repentance, if God's orientation is forgiveness, *before we say we are sorry for our sins as well as after we confess*, that means Jesus' declaration from the cross, "Father, forgive them, for they don't know what they are doing," is for everyone, good and bad. Yes, it does.

4. Doesn't this make for what Dietrich Bonhoeffer calls "cheap grace"? No, it doesn't. Grace is free, but not cheap. It cost Jesus his life to offer grace like this.

5. Jesus forgave everyone from the cross, but not everyone receives the benefits of that forgiveness. It's like a check for a million dollars is given freely, to undeserving people, but not everyone cashes it. Some ignore it. Some put it in a drawer. Some don't turn the check over and personally endorse it. Some don't appropriate what has been accomplished on the cross. Yes, grace is like receiving a check with our name on it for more money than we can imagine. All we need to do is believe in the one who gave it and personally endorse what has been given. Grace. Saving grace.

Chapter Eleven

Grace

... Because of his great love for us, God, who is rich in mercy, made us alive with Christ even when we were dead in transgressions — it is by grace you have been saved. And God raised us up with Christ and seated us with him in the heavenly realms in Christ Jesus, in order that in the coming ages he might show the incomparable riches of his grace, expressed in his kindness to us in Christ Jesus. For it is by grace you have been saved, through faith — and this not from yourselves, it is the gift of God — not of works, so that no one can boast. For we are God's workmanship, created in Christ Jesus to do good works, which God prepared in advance for us to do. — Ephesians 2:4-10*

Grace is freely given to us when we don't deserve it. Grace comes to us in the person of Jesus Christ. Grace is communicated to us through word and sacraments. Grace is God's way of changing us from enemies to friends. We are saved by grace.

Faith is our response to the grace of God in Jesus Christ. Faith is not a super good work by which we earn heaven. Faith is created in our hearts by the Holy Spirit. As Luther says in *The Small Catechism*:

> *I believe that Jesus Christ, true God, begotten of the Father from eternity, and also true man, born of the Virgin Mary, is my Lord....*

I believe that I cannot by my own reason or strength believe in Jesus Christ, my Lord, or come to him; but the Holy Ghost has called me by the Gospel, enlightened me with his gifts, sanctified and kept me in the true faith; even as he calls, gathers, enlightens and sanctifies the whole Christian Church on earth and keeps it with Jesus Christ in the one true faith....[23]

Forgiveness comes to us by the grace of God in Jesus Christ. We pass that forgiveness on to others, not because they deserve it, but because we have received it from God when we did not deserve it and he wants us to pass on what we have received. Some people have hurt us so badly that from a human point of view it's impossible for us to forgive them. Every attempt to offer forgiveness to those who don't deserve it based solely on human effort will fail. We are called to let Christ love those who have hurt us. Christ loves people, even our enemies, through us.

Actually, we can only offer forgiveness. The person who has hurt us must accept that offer before he or she will be forgiven. Often our problem is that we are afraid to offer forgiveness. From a human point of view, those who have hurt us don't deserve forgiveness. We don't want to be open to being hurt again. We don't want to give up our resentments. But as long as we hold on to our resentments, we turn other people's problems into our problems.

Grace, when the benefits are appropriated by faith, changes our attitudes. As Ephesians 2:6 says, we get transferred to heavenly places where values are turned upside down. Revenge turns to relief. Resentments turn to healing. Grace received becomes forgiveness offered, even to our enemies. Everything is transformed when we realize we are saved by grace.

"Have you read Pastor Jeff's article in the newsletter about grace, faith, and forgiveness?" Grace Livingstone asked Mary. "It sounds like 'pie in the sky by and by' to me."

"Yes, I saw it. It may be a little idealistic, but there's a lot of truth in it, Grace. What is it that bothers you about it?"

"Mary, I've never told you before; I've never told anyone. When I was twelve, my father came home drunk and raped me.

108

He doesn't believe it. I tried to talk to him about it once, but he wouldn't listen. He said it was just a bad dream I had. But I know it's true. It really happened. Am I supposed to forgive him for that?" She was crying uncontrollably.

"I'll come right over. This is important. We've got to talk." Mary set the phone down gently and prayed, *"What do you want me to say to her?"*

Thomas Livingstone had changed his mind. He decided to let the pastor stop by his house for a short talk. "This is Tom Livingstone, Grace's father," he said when he telephoned the pastor. "She said that maybe I should talk to you. I've been very sick lately. Grace said not to postpone talking to you too long because my health is so poor."

"I'll be over this afternoon at 2 p.m., if that time is okay with you," Pastor Jeff said.

"That's fine."

When the pastor sat down with Tom, he asked, "Can you tell me anything about yourself?"

"It's a bad liver problem," Tom said. "I've been a drinker all of my adult life. I've been in and out of Alcoholics Anonymous over the years. It's really a good organization. Good people who really try to help you. I've been dry for a couple of years now, but I guess all that drinking has finally caught up with me. Grace speaks so highly of you I thought it might help her if I talked to you for a little while."

"Sure, Tom. I'm glad to talk to you."

"My biggest concern is Grace. I know I don't have long to live, and there's no hope for me, but Grace is a good person. You know that bum she's been livin' with? She threw him out last week. He was just using her. She can be strong when she has to be. She's like her mother. Strong. Good and strong, like, I mean, inside.

"Grace has always been good, even when I was less than a good father. I wasn't a good husband to her mom either. I wasn't around much. Now that I'm sober, I've tried to apologize, but I don't think she has accepted it.

"There's something eating at her. She won't talk to me about it. Deep down inside, I feel she really resents me. Would you to try to talk to her and see if she can get it out? Before I die, I mean. I don't expect any miracles, but it won't be good for her if she doesn't release whatever is bothering her before I die."

"Tom, I appreciate your concern for Grace. She's been coming to church quite a bit lately, and she has completed the Pastor's class, but has said she isn't ready to join the church yet. We aren't rushing her, but there does seem to be something on her mind. Can you share anything about the family's religious background?"

"When Grace was little, we used to go to church. We never had her baptized, but she went to a Lutheran Sunday School. That was a time when I was drinkin' heavy and Marion, that's Grace's mother, had to work a lot of extra hours to keep the family together. We just drifted away from church."

"Tom, you said something when I first came in that I'd like to have you clarify if you would. You said, 'There's no hope for me.' "

"Yeah. That's true. No use trying to save a bum like me. If there's an afterlife, I'll get what I deserve, and it won't be heaven."

"All of us are sinners, Tom. Christ came to save all of us, including you."

"Sure. Sure. But you are wasting your time on me. I'm pretty set in my ways. I'm a lost cause. Let's get back to Grace. Will you try to help her?"

"Of course, Tom. I'll try."

"I hate to rush you, Pastor, but I have an AA friend comin' over in a short time, so I guess you should be on your way."

"It was good to meet you, Tom. You aren't a lost cause. There are no lost causes with God. Would you let me have a prayer with you?"

"Maybe later. Maybe another time. This religion stuff kinda' bothers me. Just try to help Grace if you can."

"It was good meeting you. Let's talk again."

"Sure. Later. Sometime later."

"Mary, thanks for coming," Grace said. "That article really upset me. I just can't forgive my father for what he did to my

110

mother. He ruined her life. I just can't forgive him for raping me. He ruined my life, too."

Mary listened. She didn't offer advice, just listened. Grace poured out her soul, crying one minute, angry the next. After an hour of expressing hurt, rage, and bitterness at her father's behavior, she calmed down.

"It's good you got all these feelings out, Grace. I hope you are at peace now."

"But I still hate my father for what he did."

"When you are ready, we can talk about forgiveness."

"Forgiveness? I don't think so! Even if he repents, I don't think I can forgive him for what he did! And he won't repent! He never says he's sorry for anything! The only thing he's ever sorry for is that he got caught! He always blames someone else for what goes wrong. He never accepts responsibility. What makes you think he will repent now?"

"God help me," Mary prayed. "Even if he never repents, you can offer forgiveness to him in your heart. That way you won't make his problem your problem. You have no control over whether or not he will be forgiven. That's up to him and God. The only thing you have control over is the offer of forgiveness. Until you offer forgiveness, you will continue to be troubled."

"You sound like Pastor Jeff. Even if you're right, I can't do it. It's too hard after what he's done."

"Try to think about what Christ has done for you."

"I'll try, but I don't think I'll ever be able to forgive him."

After 45 minutes, John, Tom's AA friend said, "Tom, you don't look so good. You're pale. You look sick."

"Maybe I should take a nap."

"Maybe you should see a doctor."

"Maybe later."

As the friend started to let himself out, he heard a thud. Tom was on the floor. John called 911. The ambulance took Tom to the emergency ward. John phoned Grace from the hospital. "Your dad is in the hospital," he said. "He fell to the floor as I was leaving.

His stomach is hard and swollen. They say he's in a coma. You'd better come right up."

"Dad," Grace whispered in Tom's ear, "can you hear me?" Tom didn't respond. He died three days later.

At the funeral, Pastor Jeff talked about his visit at Tom's home the day he was taken to the hospital. He shared Tom's concern for his daughter without going into the details of what worried Tom. He also talked about the fact that Christ died for all sinners and that we never know when a person repents for his sins. He tried to comfort Grace in every way he could.

After the graveside service, Grace told the pastor, "I just can't believe it. He was fine the morning I saw him. I never got another chance to talk to him. Now it's too late."

When nearly everyone had left the graveyard, Grace stood staring at the grave, thinking: *Too late to tell him I loved him in spite of all his faults. Too late to tell him I was willing to forgive him for what he did to Mom and me. Too late to show him that my life is changing for the better. Too late to tell him that God has come into my life. Too late to tell him Jesus died for his sins. Too late. Too late.*

As if reading Grace's mind, Mary who was standing nearby said, "You are probably thinking it's too late to get reconciled with your dad. It isn't. If you mean it, you can still tell God that you are willing to forgive your dad. He will take care of the rest." Later that day, Mary phoned Grace and read some Bible verses to her.

That night, Grace prayed into her tear-soaked pillow, *Dear Father, I'm new at this stuff, but I can't handle the resentment and hatred anymore. It's too much for me to carry. I give it up to you. I believe; help my unbelief.*

Questions For Personal Consideration
And/Or Group Discussion

1. Re-read Ephesians 2:4-10. What does it mean?

2. If you read Pastor Jeff's article in your church newsletter, what would you think of it?

3. What does it mean to appropriate what has already been accomplished by Christ?

4. How would you try to comfort and help a woman who was raped by her father?

5. Do you see any signs of repentance in Tom's conversation with the pastor?

6. How would you address Tom's statement that he was a bum not worth trying to save?

7. What can Pastor Jeff or Mary do to try to help Grace?

8. Comment on the statement, "God allows U-turns."

Digging Deeper

1. Forgiveness is the one thing needful and the hardest thing of all. It is needful because without it we remain un-reconciled to others. It is the hardest thing of all because we don't want to expose ourselves to getting hurt again by those who hurt us. When others who have hurt us don't repent for what they have done, that adds coals to the burning fire of resentments in our hearts. Even if they repent, it seems too easy for them to get by with just saying, "I'm sorry."

2. Jesus said, "You have heard that it was said, 'Love your neighbor and hate your enemy.' But I tell you: Love your enemies and pray for those who persecute you, that you may be sons of your Father in heaven. He causes his sun to rise on the evil and the good, and sends rain on the righteous and the unrighteous. If you love those who love you, what reward will you get? Are not even the tax collectors doing that? And if you greet only your brothers, what are you doing more than others? Do not even pagans do that? Be perfect, therefore, as your heavenly Father is perfect" (Matthew 5:43-48).

3. "Perfect" in Matthew 5:48 doesn't mean without error. The Greek word behind our English translation is *telos* which means "whole, mature or complete." What Jesus is saying here is that we can't love our enemies unless we are whole like our heavenly Father is whole, not getting trapped in demonic fragmentation. Receiving Holy Communion is one of God's ways to make us whole, helping us get a heavenly picture of what is happening on earth. We can offer forgiveness even to those who don't deserve it only when we realize we have been forgiven by God when we didn't deserve it.

4. Romans 12:17-21 says: "Do not repay anyone evil for evil. Be careful to do what is right in the eyes of everybody. If it is possible as far as it depends on you, live at peace with everyone. Do not take revenge, my friends, but leave room for God's wrath, for it is written: 'It is mine to avenge; I will repay,' says the Lord. On the contrary: 'If your enemy is hungry, feed him; if he is thirsty, give him something to drink. In doing this, you will heap burning coals on his head.' Do not be overcome by evil, but overcome evil with good."

Chapter Twelve

Hope

"... I know the plans I have for you," declares the
*LORD, "plans to prosper you and not to harm you,
plans to give you hope and a future."*
— Jeremiah 29:11

The original context of this passage was the Babylonian Captivity of the Jews. It was a letter to the Jewish exiles in Babylon. In
586 B.C., they were captured by Nebuchadnezzar and deported to
a foreign land. They were defeated, discouraged, depressed, and
dislocated. Jeremiah predicted that after seventy years in Babylon,
God would restore them to good fortune and return them to the
Promised Land. "I have plans for you," God says, "plans to give
you hope and a future."

The original context of these words was the captivity of God's
people in ancient Babylon. But there is an additional context for
these words of hope: your life and mine.

Conflict comes. Troubles. Feelings of estrangement. A longing for some unknown home. We seem to be captives of something — demonic forces too strong for us, demonic forces around
us ... within us. We are captives, each and every one of us.

God's word applies to us as well as to the ancient Jews to whom
it was written. Like them, we have our times of defeat, discourage-
ment, depression, and dislocation. In such times we are ready to
give up. *Why try?* we ask in the innermost parts of our souls. *How
can we sing songs of hope when we are in a foreign land?*

117

The Jews in captivity felt the same way. Can you identify with their pathos, their longing, their groaning?

> *By the rivers of Babylon —*
> > *there we sat down and wept*
> > *when we remembered Zion.*
> *On the willows there*
> > *we hung up our harps.*
> *For there our captors*
> > *asked us for songs,*
> > *and our tormentors asked for mirth, saying,*
> > *"Sing us one of the songs of Zion!"*
>
> *How could we sing the LORD's song*
> > *in a foreign land?*
> > > — Psalm 137:1-4 (NRSV)

In this context of sorrow the people of God remembered the message from God. "I know the plans I have for you, plans to prosper you and not to harm you, plans to give you hope and a future." In our times of sorrow, we too can remember a word from God with our names on it. The message reads: "I have plans for you. Hope again. I have a future for you."

It is precisely at these low times, when we feel like hanging our happiness on the weeping willows, that God's word can give us hope. It is precisely at times of dislocation that we can discover that our true home is with our heavenly Father. We are in a far away country. Yes, but those who know they are lost really listen when God calls.

When our strength gives out, we can discover the invitation to come home through Jesus Christ. In Christ there is strength from God. It is precisely at these times that we discover for the first time, or perhaps rediscover, what it means to be a child of God for whom Jesus died on the cross. Jesus died for us when we were sinners and deserved nothing but punishment. He died so we can return home to God.

It is precisely at the darkest moments of dislocation when there seems to be no hope and we hit rock bottom that we can discover the Rock of Ages. The worst time sometimes becomes the best time because in the worst time we can learn to depend entirely on God, not ourselves. In the worst time we can discover grace, God's gift to sinners. God's grace is for you. It restores you to your journey home.

A man recently told me that he was weeping uncontrollably at the grave of his father when the pastor read these words, "... Here we do not have an enduring city, but we are looking for the city that is to come" (Hebrews 13:14). "Changed my life," he said. "Got my mind relocated on the heavenly home God has prepared for those who love him. This world seemed so important until I began to think, really think, about the world to come. That's when I woke up to the reality of God. It was a defining moment."

When the bottom drops out and depression steps in and takes control, remember these words, "I know the plans I have for you ... a hope and a future." When demonic forces take you where you don't want to go, remember Babylon was such a place, a passage point on the way back to Zion. In New Testament terms, Calvary was just a brief stopover on the way to freedom. When you get to the end of your rope, tie a knot and hang onto these words from God: "I know the plans I have for you, plans to prosper you and not to harm you." Babylonian Captivity is not a good place to be, but it is only a temporary dislocation on the way back to the Promised Land.

God sends us a message from eternity. "I have plans for you ... and a future." Hope can be restored if we believe this message. Hope is to the soul what oxygen is to the body. We really can't live without it. Hope springs eternal when we turn to the Eternal One. When we come to Holy Communion, we turn to the Eternal One.

When we come to Holy Communion we receive a foretaste of the feast to come in the kingdom of God. In the kingdom of God, hope turns to sight. "Now we see but a poor reflection as in a mirror; then we shall see face to face. Now I know in part; then I shall know fully, even as I am fully known" (1 Corinthians 13:12).

Hear these words of hope: "This is the body and blood of Christ given and shed for you." We live in a fallen world, but we receive a word from on high: "I have plans for you. I have hope for you. I have a future for you." In Holy Communion we taste the kingdom bread, the bread of heaven. We taste "tomorrow's bread" today.[24]

We live in this world, but we are not of this world. We belong to the Lord. Our eternal home is with God. In, through, and under the bread and wine of Holy Communion we get a preview of coming attractions. Therefore, though we live in a fallen world, we can have hope.

Saint Paul speaks of hope in the context of the fallen world. He puts it this way:

> *... The creation itself will be liberated from its bondage to decay and brought into the glorious freedom of the children of God. We know that the whole creation has been groaning as in the pains of childbirth right up to the present time. Not only so, but we ourselves, who have the firstfruits of the Spirit, groan inwardly as we wait eagerly for our adoption as sons, the redemption of our bodies. For in this hope we are saved. But hope that is seen is no hope at all. Who hopes for what he already has? But if we hope for what we do not yet have, we wait for it patiently. In the same way, the Spirit helps us in our weakness.*
> — Romans 8:21-26

Saint Paul goes on to encourage us to believe the Scriptures and have hope in God.

> *For everything that was written in the past was written to teach us, so that through endurance and the encouragement of the Scriptures we might have hope.*
> — Romans 15:4

Then Saint Paul offers us a benediction of hope.

May the God of hope fill you with all joy and peace as
you trust in him, so that you may overflow with hope
by the power of the Holy Spirit.   — Romans 15:13

Grace watched as Pastor Jeff closed the Bible on the pulpit and took his seat. The church was so quiet you could hear a pin drop. Grace was thinking, *"Dad just died. He wasn't perfect, far from it, but he was still my dad. Now I must go on without him. Is it possible that I could actually get a new Father?"*

When it came time for Holy Communion, Grace went forward with Mary. She listened and watched carefully. She knew she couldn't receive Communion yet since she had not been baptized, but Mary had urged her to come forward for a blessing. She heard the pastor bless a child next to her, saying, "Remember your Baptism." Then it was her turn. She bowed her head. The pastor put his hand on her head, came close to her ear and said, "Remember, Grace, Jesus died for you on the cross, to set you free."

Jesus died for me on the cross. Why have I struggled against accepting it? Why have I doubted so much? Why have I been so unwilling to trust God? Can I really accept the fact that Christ accepts me when I am unacceptable? I'm afraid that would change me. Wouldn't that change be for the better? Why are you cast down, O my soul? Hope. Hope in God.

For the benediction that day, Pastor Jeff used Romans 15:13. "May the God of hope, fill you with all joy and peace as you trust in him, so that you may overflow with hope by the power of the Holy Spirit."

Questions For Personal Consideration
And/Or Group Discussion

1. Do you plan ahead a lot or do you generally make decisions on the spur of the moment?

2. What are the benefits of these two different styles?

3. What difference did it make to the Jews in exile in Babylon that God had a plan for their future?

4. What difference does it make for you that God has a plan for your future?

5. What difference does it make that God has a plan for your church?

6. What difference does hope make in the life of a person or a church?

7. Does God actually allow U-turns?

Digging Deeper

1. In the Lord's Prayer we pray, "Give us this day our daily bread." An alternate translation is "Give us today tomorrow's bread." Some modern versions of the Bible offer this alternate translation as a footnote. "Tomorrow's bread" is the bread of the kingdom which we can receive today in the sacrament of Holy Communion.

   The kingdom of God doesn't come in fullness until the end of time, but Jesus expected his followers to live as if the kingdom was already here. For example, since the kingdom has burst in upon us (in part) in the coming of Jesus, we are called to forgive those who hurt us, even though they are not deserving, just like God forgives us when we are not deserving.

   The meaning of praying for "tomorrow's bread" today is that if we are to live like the people of God in the here and now, we need kingdom bread, manna from heaven, to strengthen us. We are unable to be kingdom people without kingdom bread.

Is it possible that Jesus had this in mind when he taught his disciples to pray this petition? (*See Abba: Another Look At The Lord's Prayer* by Ron Lavin, CSS Publishing Company, Lima, Ohio, 2003.)

2. In Romans 8:23, Saint Paul speaks of "firstfruits." The Greek word behind our English translation is *arroban*. *Arroban* means previews, foretaste, deposit, or firstfruits. Since Christians have this *arroban*, we groan inwardly for the fullness of the kingdom of God and overflow with hope so that others may be touched by it (Romans 15:13).

"... It is by grace you have been saved...."
— Ephesians 2:8

Epilogue

"That was quite a birthday party!" Mary Anderson said with enthusiasm. "Can you believe that you are sixty years old?"

"It's hard to believe. Seems just like yesterday when Sarah Williams introduced me to you. For thirty years now we've been friends. We've had lots of highs and lots of lows. We've shared them all."

"Let me help you clean up."

"That isn't necessary. Bud can help me."

"In case you missed it, your husband is taking a nap on the front-room couch. Don't wake him. I'll help you. I may be 75, but I'm no slouch when it comes to cleaning up after a party."

"You're no slouch at anything you set your mind to do. You never cease to amaze me. Do you remember thirty years ago how you had to keep after me when I was adrift? You sure were persistent."

"I hope I wasn't too pushy."

"There is a difference between persistent and pushy. You are persistent, not pushy."

"Thanks. It wasn't easy for me to become a Christian. I figured it must have been hard for you to overcome your problems too."

"Remember that guy Jake I finally threw out of my house?" Grace whispered. "I never could have done that without your support. And when my dad died. I thought I never would come out of that strange mixture of grief and anger. You were there. Listening and helping."

"That's what friends are for."

"You are a friend, the best friend I have ever had."

"I feel the same way."

"Do you remember how I struggled before I finally agreed to be baptized? Poor Pastor Jeff. He tried everything. He counseled with me. He listened to me. He tried to get me into therapy. None of it worked. What worked was your persistent faithfulness to me."

"I couldn't have done it without Pastor Jeff. He was a good preacher and teacher. He was a good friend. Wasn't that special that he flew in from Minneapolis for your party today? What a surprise that was!"

"Knocked my socks off. And that prayer he said before dinner. I'll never forget it. He may be retired, but he still talks to God like he's just an old friend. Over the years we've seen quite a few pastors come and go at Messiah Church, but Pastor Jeff is still my favorite. He always made Communion seem so personal. He and you and Sarah kept after me when I was going through tough times. Think about it ... my life would have never changed if I had not nearly run down that dear sweet old lady, Sarah Williams."

"She was one special Christian woman, one of the real saints God put on earth to help us all. She was kind and comforting, but she was also tough when she had to be. That's a rare and special combination. Even after thirty years, I miss her."

"You are a lot like her, you know."

"That's the nicest thing anyone has ever said about me."

"Speaking of tough old ladies, do you remember that tape by Gert Behanna you gave me thirty years ago? I still have it. I played it again the other day. I love the way she ended her talk with a prayer. I use that prayer all the time.

O Lord, I ain't what I ought to be.
And, Lord, I ain't what I'm gonna be.
But thanks, Lord.
I ain't what I used to be.

"I love that prayer. Recently I came across a story in a Christian magazine about another loving, but tough old lady. We're done with the dishes. Why don't I put on a pot of tea and I'll read it to you?"

126

"Good idea," Mary said, smiling at the way Grace had grown in faith.

"I'll get the article. I have it in my purse," Grace said with a smile.

Watch Out For Little Old Ladies
By Gwynn Runyard

Betty Dobbs was 79. She parked her car in the supermarket lot and was surprised how crowded it was today. Locking her car carefully she sallied forth into the store. After completing her purchases she left with a small grocery sack over her arm and made sure she had her keys at the ready. This was a practice her son had instilled in her, to always hold her keys in her right hand and if anyone accosted her, she would have a weapon with which to gouge out the assailant's eyes.

Well, she had a weapon all right, she had recently purchased a small hand gun which was now hidden in her purse. Having taken a Safety Gun Course many years ago, Betty felt quite safe and happy about her actions. No one was going to get the better of her.

As she approached the car she did a double take. Was that someone sitting in the front seat? Wait, no, not just one but two men were sitting in her front seat!

"How dare they sit in my car like that?" she muttered. Again feeling the bulge in her purse she approached the car, rapped her keys on the passenger side window and said, "Hey you, get out of the car."

The man looked up, then kept on talking as he turned to his companion. Betty was not going to have any of that nonsense. She strode around to the driver's side, and wrapped again on the window with her car keys.

"Come on, you two, out, out of the car" — again the same response greeted her. The men kept on talking and not moving. Betty thought that she would give them one more chance, because this was a serious situation and she

127

did not want to be irresponsible. She needed to give the thieves an opportunity to vacate, after all she was not a violent woman. She was just a very determined one. Again she knocked on the window, again she told them to get out, and again the response was the same. *Well,* she thought, *here goes.*

Pulling the gun from her bag she tapped the window with the barrel, but before she could say the magic words, the men were scrambling out of the car as fast as they could and making a hasty retreat.

"Hurrah!" muttered Betty as she climbed into the car, there to sit a minute to collect her thoughts and emotions, and to say a big thank you for not having to use the gun, now safely away in her bag, the safety still on.

After a few minutes Betty felt calmer. "Oh, I really should report those men to the police," she murmured, as she tried to start the car.

Whatever is the matter, she mused. *They are the right keys, aren't they? Yes, they were her car keys, but they just would not fit into the car's ignition.*

"Oh, my!" exclaimed Betty. "That is strange. That's never happened before." She leaned forward to check the glove compartment. Inside were things she had never seen before.

"Oh, my!" she whispered again. "This is not my car."

Hurriedly leaving the scene, she looked across the rows of cars and there in the next aisle sat her car, patiently waiting her return. With her grocery bag and purse over her shoulder, her keys in her hand, she unlocked the door, checked the glove compartment, and yes, everything was in the right place, and the keys fit.

Now she really must find a policeman to tell him about those men, for she knew they were planning to steal someone else's car, otherwise they would not have run off like that.

As she was leaving she noticed several security guards and honked and waved to get their attention.

She called out to them, "I need to tell you nice men about something that happened to me."

One of the guards replied: "Lady, we don't have time to chat. There's a little old lady with a pistol out in the parking lot hijacking cars!"[25]

Doubled up with laughter, Mary almost fell off the kitchen chair. "That's a good one," she said. "A really good story. Sounds like Sarah. What an indomitable gal she was. Once when Sarah and I had a disagreement about something, I said to her, 'Sarah, you are just too stubborn for your own good.' She never blinked. She just said, 'You are stubborn. I'm indomitable.' "

The longtime friends had another good laugh.

Grace was quiet for a moment. "It is good to laugh. When I was lost, I seldom laughed."

"You were lost back then, but sometimes only the lost listen, Grace. Jesus always loved lost souls. You may have been lost, but you listened to God's word. More important, you accepted what God was saying about accepting you when you weren't acceptable. That's what the grace of God is all about. Sarah taught me that. She also said, 'After the lost listen to God, then they can laugh, the full, hearty laugh of the redeemed. Since the Devil never laughs, a sense of humor is one of the best weapons in our fight against evil.' "

"That's quite a statement. It sounds like Sarah. I believe it. Sarah was a strong Christian woman. It's good to remember her. I just realized that it is thirty years ago tomorrow that I almost ran her down in front of the church. What a different life I have now because of that accident."

Mary was quiet for a moment. Then she said, "Sometimes I think there are no accidents, just incidents to which God adds his grace."

That night Grace prayed:

Father, thank you for my special sixtieth birthday party. Thanks for guiding my life these sixty years. Thanks for my wonderful husband, Bud. Thanks for Mary, for

Sarah, and for Pastor Jeff and all the other Christians who changed my life.

Father, through Jesus you made me a new person. My past no longer controls me. Help me to find other lost souls and witness to those who see themselves only through their rearview mirrors like I used to.

In Jesus' holy name. Amen.

Tips For Pastors, Group Leaders, And Teachers

Below find seven tips for pastors who use the material in this book for instruction classes for new members, for teachers of adult classes, and for group leaders of small groups.

1. Start and/or end each study with prayer.

2. For the best results, when used in classes or group study, all participants should have copies of *Saving Grace*. This is especially true since this book uses the story of Grace Livingstone to make the theology of the word and sacraments more reader friendly.

3. Use the questions at the end of each chapter as discussion starters or for personal reflection.

4. As time allows, use Digging Deeper at the end of each chapter to enrich the study and suggest application.

5. *Saving Grace* may be used by classes or groups meeting weekly, every other week, or monthly. At the beginning of each session, it will be helpful to remind the group of the main points and story line about Grace Livingstone from the previous chapter.

6. Rather than lecturing to people, try to get members of the class or group involved in the discussion of the topics. Participation results in increased retention.

7. One of the ways to get people involved in participation is to use small group techniques. Many of these techniques, as well as information on starting small groups and keeping them going, are found in *Way To Grow! Dynamic Church Growth*

Through Small Groups by Ron Lavin, CSS Publishing Company, Lima, Ohio, 1996. This book and others by Ron Lavin may be ordered by using the information below:

CSS Publishing Company
517 South Main Street
P. O. Box 4503
Lima, Ohio 45802-4503

1-800-537-1030

e-mail: orders@csspub.com

fax: 1-419-228-9184

Endnotes

Chapter One
1. The term "word" (or "word of God") will not be capitalized unless it refers to the person of Jesus.

2. *The New International Version* (NIV) capitalizes the Word when the term refers to Jesus, as it does here in John, chapter 1.

Chapter Two
3. Brennan Manning, *Abba's Child* (Colorado Springs, Colorado: NavPress 1994), pp. 126-128.

Chapter Three
4. Deuteronomy 30:14.

5. Isaiah 28:16.

6. Joel 2:82.

7. Isaiah 52:7.

8. Isaiah 53:7.

9. Alan Richardson, editor, *The Theological Word Book Of The Bible* (New York: The Macmillan Company, 1959), p. 219.

10. *Ibid.*, p. 220.

11. *Ibid.*

Chapter Four
12. Habakkuk 2:4.

Chapter Five
13. To distinguish between the sacrament of Baptism and other kinds of baptisms, I use the lower case for everything other than the sacrament of Baptism.

14. *Ibid.*

15. *Ibid.*

16. John Davies, Henry Gehman, *The Westminster Dictionary Of The Bible* (Philadelphia: Westminster Press, 1944), p. 59.

17. *Ibid.*

Chapter Six
18. The earliest manuscripts and some other ancient witness do not have Mark 16:9-30.

19. Alan Richardson, *op. cit.*, p. 219.

Chapter Eight
20. William Barclay, *The Letters To The Corinthians* (Philadelphia: Westminster Press, 1956), pp. 152-153.

Chapter Nine
21. *Ibid.*, pp. 104-105.

Chapter Ten
22. See *Stories To Remember: Another Look At The Parables Of Jesus*, by Ron Lavin (Lima, Ohio: CSS Publishing Company, 2002).

Chapter Eleven
23. Martin Luther, *Book Of Concord*, "The Small Catechism," explanation of the Second and Third Articles of the Apostles' Creed, (St. Louis, Missouri: Concordia, 1957), p. 11.

Chapter Twelve
24. For further explanation of "tomorrow's bread today" see *Abba: Another Look At The Lord's Prayer* by Ron Lavin, (Lima, Ohio: CSS Publishing Company, 2003).

Epilogue
25. Unpublished story by Gwen Tremain Runyard, used by permission of the author.

www.ingramcontent.com/pod-product-compliance
Lightning Source LLC
LaVergne TN
LVHW021511080426
835509LV00018B/2477